SANCTUARY

LIVING YOUR BEST LIFE AT HOME

SANCTUARY

LIVING YOUR BEST LIFE AT HOME

ACPbooks

make your home a sanctuary

Your step quickens, your mood lifts and you relax when you return home after a hard day's work. A glance reveals everything you hold dear. Home is a special place for you, your family and your friends. This is a place to refresh and reinvigorate your spirit and body, preparing you for whatever your world brings. ~ Create a sanctuary filled with your favourite things; with artworks or family photos that bring a smile to your face. Find a sacred space that's just your own, where you can empty your mind and find stillness. Bathe away the concerns of a busy day in your bathroom. Then step into a calming bedroom and relax into a good night's sleep. ~ But enjoying your home as a sanctuary is not a solitary experience. The love and support of family and friends is there to be shared. Gather in the kitchen, the deck or the garden to enjoy good food and conversation, and reinforce those important connections to each other. ~ Finally, bring the very best of the world home. Leave your sanctuary for a little while and recharge your interests by discovering new cultures and new experiences to enrich your life. It will make your home an even more wonderful place to be.

CONTENTS

UNWIND &
IMAGINE

Your home is a place where you should feel completely relaxed and secure. Nesting and cocooning have become buzzwords in recent times and it's not without reason. A house envelops its owners in warmth and familiarity. It should be a stress-free, pleasurable place – welcoming, calming and filled with personal treasures. ~ Approaching your home at the end of the day should bring a palpable sense of relief and comfort. As your footsteps pick up, your heart becomes that bit lighter – soon, you'll be at your own front door. Inside is your refuge from the world. This space, your space, is sacred. ~ You should be able to shut the door behind you and be at ease, and a considered composition of colours, textures, fabrics and accessories will help achieve this. ~ It's time to unwind and imagine … and to begin creating your sanctuary.

FRONT OF HOUSE

1 The journey into your sanctuary should be a gentle one. The stepping-stone path to this cottage winds through a well-composed garden of contrasting foliage. The large pale pavers are easy to see in low light – an important consideration when laying a path. The garden is a relaxed rather than formal design, and adds a sense of welcome.

2 An installation artwork at the front of your home will lift your spirits every time you see it. The sculpture in this front garden appears to herald arrivals with a trumpet. Its tall form is in harmony with the conifers nearby. A water feature can also add interest and movement to an entrance.

previous page
Sunshine plays off softly coloured natural stone and timber in this airy entrance area. An internal courtyard brings light and air deep into this tropical home, and the absence of fussy decorating lends it tranquillity.

You long to be home after a hard day's work

MAKE A WONDERFUL WELCOME

The journey into your abode starts before the front door. That first impression from the street is often retained the longest. As any real estate agent will confirm, street appeal sells, but it also communicates a welcome. That metaphorical welcome mat is felt in the way you present your house, from streetscape to foyer.

Good landscaping draws the eye to your front door and a well-finished driveway and path easily direct you inside. Good external lighting – either on timers or with motion detectors – is essential. As well as letting you see where you're putting your feet, lighting transforms a house at night from a looming presence to an inviting place.

Plantings are important. Your home may suggest a landscaping style; white river stones and architectural plants such as succulents and cycads work well with contemporary homes, while cottagey plants and herbaceous borders suit more traditional houses. Avoid having hard, spiky plants right next to walkways as they could cause injury.

A garden's fragrances are important, too. Plants such as lemon-scented geraniums and groundcovers like creeping thyme and oregano may be put in near a path so they release their fragrance as your visitors walk in. The scents of eucalyptus, orange jessamine (*Murraya paniculata*) and jasmine are distinctive and memorable.

Creating a sense of welcome doesn't mean abandoning privacy; a fence will define the point where your home starts. However, trees or fences that obscure the view to your front door and windows could provide cover for burglars and create a security risk.

Your home's front door can have a big effect. Research suggests that the larger and more impressive the front door, the greater the perceived value of a house. A front door finished in a warm colour or with glass panes that break up its bulk is much more engaging than a huge timber slab. And there should be a knocker or doorbell so visitors can announce their presence without rapping their knuckles on the door.

Inside, the entrance area should immediately make you feel at home. As little time is actually spent here, feel free to be dramatic with bold colours, sculptures and artwork. Lighting should smooth the transition inside with a soft glow rather than a strong beam. Having a place for coats and keys will also make entrances (and exits) easier.

A house should always smell good. Open the windows and air out your dwelling every day, and deodorise carpets and rugs regularly to extinguish any lingering odours from pets. To bring in a lovely aroma, burn incense or use an oil-burner.

You should create a home that appeals to all your senses. It takes more than a doormat to spell out a message of welcome – a thoughtful approach from streetside to entrance will make you and your guests always feel at home.

1 A more formal garden design suits this late-Victorian house. The overall effect is of cool green leaves and white blooms, although closer inspection reveals a smattering of pink and purple flowers among the foliage. The white gravel path reflects the sunshine, dispelling any hint of gloom from the dark stone house.

2 A garden urn awash with white petunias is the focal point of the front yard. Buxus hedges border garden beds where hydrangeas, agapanthus, camellias and Acanthus mollis flourish and roses are underplanted with native violets.

The entrance area in your home can be a place for bold decorating and displaying

1 *Slabs of black granite float above a riverbed of pebbles in this imposing foyer, where cool-coloured walls are an effective backdrop for sculptures. The double-height void is well suited to displaying artworks, as there is room to stand back and admire their form. The decor is strictly minimalist, relying on the inherent texture of the building materials for effect, yet the generosity of the space gives a feeling of luxury.*

2 *Large wooden doors transform this entrance hall into a series of intimate chambers, with the final door revealing the main bedroom. While the rich earthy tones are consistent, using different types of flooring makes the hall feel less like a thoroughfare and more like a room. The notion of each room as a destination can be enhanced by positioning artwork to face the doorway.*

loved collectables   HALLWAYS

ARTWORKS & COLLECTABLES

Anything is collectable, from art to antique books to teaspoons, and almost everyone is a collector to some degree. When you put that collection out on show, what you're really sharing with the world is your passion.

The room where your collection is displayed should have some relevance: a china collection in the dining room or antique dolls in a bedroom. Respect the time and money put into your collection by housing it in a worthy cabinet or shelving system, lit to make it a centre of attention. (If a collection is spread haphazardly throughout the home, it soon loses its impact.) For their protection, keep the pieces out of strong sunlight and make sure that where they're displayed is free of damp or mould.

An artwork is often chosen as a form of self-expression, so revel in the process of finding a piece that you connect with. A piece of art brings colour, atmosphere and depth to a room and personalises a living space in a way that little else can.

While collections often relate to a specific room, art can essentially 'create' a room by providing the theme and colour scheme for furnishings. A cushion may be used to pick up a colour in an artwork, or a blond timber dining table may provide a contrast to a dark and moody painting. If you're adding art as a finishing touch, pare back your room to the basics and then reintroduce each element, from rugs to armchairs, to find the perfect colour and textural balance.

Allow your artwork room to breathe, especially if it's bright. Black-and-white works draw in the eye more, so require less blank wall around them. When hanging artworks or photos, find the horizontal midline of the work and position it so that it's in your line of sight when you're standing.

An artwork can inspire a distinct mood, so try living with the artwork before fixing it in place. You may well find that a dark, intense painting is unsuitable to hang in a room where you usually rest and unwind but will work well in an entrance area.

Art for the home is not restricted to original works. You can display posters, sketches, photographs and prints of all shapes and sizes. A skilled picture framer can turn even swatches of fabric, old letters or poems into pieces to decorate your walls.

Sculptural works may be displayed on a shelf or a plinth. Yet even a Marc Newson dish rack, Philippe Starck juicer or classic Alvar Aalto vase are beautiful enough to be regarded as art, so place them somewhere that reflects their status.

Remember, appropriate accent lighting gives art more presence. A spotlight, halogen downlight, lamp or small 'art light' can be used to highlight a work.

Try to think of your home as a 'living gallery' and how you can make your art pieces look their best. White walls generally work well with contemporary art, while classical-style pictures look glorious against a red background. Dark walls are suited to elaborate gilt frames, and glossy photographs gain more depth against textured backgrounds such as brickwork or rough plaster.

It's the beautiful extras you place in your home that serve to make it your own. In a sanctuary you have the luxury to celebrate your passions and personal style, so take advantage of this and prove that home is where the art is.

1 What's around the corner? Use a hallway to pique curiosity by framing views of eye-catching artwork, such as this Zimbabwean sculpture. A series of doors and panels of rich American walnut also help to direct interest through this house. The flow is maintained by the tonal layering of walnut, ochre and chocolate.

2 This wide hallway displays a collection of modern artworks. Internal walls are the best place to hang paintings to avoid mould, so this hallway makes an ideal gallery. Old and new are deftly combined. The plasterwork, stained glass and archway are typical period features, while the light fitting in the hallway is wildly contemporary.

3 As little time is actually spent in a vestibule it can afford to be overstated. This is a place to indulge in the theatrical, bold, colourful or quirky. This foyer reflects a French-influenced opulence, featuring ornamental columns, arched niches and a prized collection of antiques and china.

LIVING ROOMS

The living

1 *Be inspired by your home's architecture, not restricted by it. In this home a very simple colour scheme mediates the mix of traditional and modern. Period-style skirtings and plasterwork are made modish with a coat of white paint and provide a plain backdrop for a new-fashioned chaise longue and flokati-style rug. It's an uncluttered look, but not an uncomfortable one. This is a place to simply stop and breathe in a busy day.*

2 *Using textures in a scheme, rather than pattern and colour, makes a room seem more peaceful and unhurried. Natural materials like stone and timber bring a subtle visual interest to a neutral-toned setting. Here, the hard surfaces are softened with a smile-inducing shag-pile rug and sectional lounge suite.*

room is the first place you turn to unwind, let go of stress and reconnect with home

USING TEXTURE IN THE HOME

The way something feels satisfies our emotions at the deepest level. The youngest baby responds to touch, nuzzling into its parents to feel safe and secure. Even when you're grown up there is intense delight in snuggling up in soft wool.

Yet texture's effect is not restricted to touch. The contrast of knobbly and smooth also works on a visual level, making a decorating scheme look much more interesting than when all the surfaces have the same finish. Neutral schemes, which have become so popular in recent years, rely on textures to avoid seeming flat and boring.

A room's mood is heavily influenced by the textures within it. Pose the question: How do I wish to feel in this room? The living room is a place to unwind and let go of stress, so hard, cold surfaces are out of place here – they won't allow for the relaxation you seek. Likewise, bedrooms should be filled with things that are soft and soothing. A dining room, on the other hand, is a place for conversation and socialising; colours and finishes that stimulate the senses are at home here.

Floors and walls provide the biggest sweep of colour and texture in a room. If you wish to create a calming environment, jute, sisal or hardwood floors are ideal. More formal spaces will shine with tiles or polished concrete. Thick carpets or Persian rugs are soft underfoot and also add visual softness to a space.

Walls may be painted to have a smooth matt look or in suede, pearlescent or metallic finishes that bring a visual texture to their surface. Wallpaper, exposed brick, render and tile also have their own pattern and texture.

Of course, too much texture and pattern can induce visual overload. Where walls are highly textured, keep floors smooth and vice versa. An intricately woven carpet loses clout when placed against walls of exposed brick or extravagant wallpaper. Just a touch of texture, say, a woven timber screen, may be enough in your scheme.

Contrast is the key. Matt walls are great with patterned glass, while glossy walls can offset velvet upholstery. A chalky matt ceiling will play up cornices painted in a glossy trim, or a feature wall with a metallic sheen. And an exposed brick wall becomes an industrial-style feature when teamed with stainless steel and glass furniture.

Furniture provides a kaleidoscope of surfaces with which to play the contrast game: timber, glass, stainless steel and wicker. Upholstery, window treatments, cushions and throws are also there for the mixing. Even a single accent cushion or table runner can soften the feel of a room. A woollen throw over a wicker chair, or a stack of towels against the tiles in a bathroom will provide instant warmth.

The texture of fabrics helps define the nature of each room. In the bedroom, smooth satin, silk and luscious faux fur will establish the seductive mood of a love lair. In the dining room, a more formal feel can be created by using heavy fabrics like damask against smooth timber. You may want to envelop your home with a generous mix of light and heavy fabrics such as sheers and velvets, linens, wool and cotton. You'll also find that natural fibres of cotton, hemp and wool are a great base against which you can contrast synthetic fabrics like viscose, rayon or polyester.

So forget colour for a moment and mix and match furnishings with a focus on texture. Touch plays a vital role in connecting you with your surroundings and different textures can make that experience all the more pleasurable.

When you sink into your sofa you're aware that a texture's effect is not limited

1 Furnished with soft upholstered chairs, a lush carpet and a subtle colour scheme, this living room is indeed serene. The woollen throws and plump cushions add to the comfort, while the ornate gilt frame on the mirror brings a little more luxury to the scheme.

2 Make the living room a place of contentment by keeping it at a comfortable temperature. Fresh air is welcomed into this room through concertina doors, and if the mercury rises there are overhead fans to cool things down. In winter the doors are closed and a fire keeps the space cosy.

3 Your choice of artwork and collectables reflects who you are – it's all about surrounding yourself with those things that you are passionate about. This home revels in a global fusion of styles. Many of the artworks were gathered on the owners' travels and no doubt inspire many more adventures.

4 Fire played a vital role in human survival, and while there are now more efficient ways to cook and to heat your home, its presence still brings comfort. This fireplace, set in a stone-faced chimney, is a gathering place for a modern household. Gazing into the flames is guaranteed to help you unwind.

to touch; it also has visual appeal

WINDOW DRESSINGS

Curtains have returned to favour after a decade of either bare windows, timber venetians or plantation shutters. The trend today is for simple drops of sheer fabrics that are teamed with roll-down blinds to control light and glare.

There are three reasons for dressing windows: privacy, beauty and insulation. Glass is a poor insulator, with up to 24 per cent of a home's heat lost through windows in winter, and too much pulled in during summer. Lined curtains and blinds are a simple way to tame heat and glare, and also keep things warmer in winter.

When you're decorating your home, decide on the mood you wish to create and choose your window coverings accordingly. A beautiful view may be enhanced with a simple arrangement of floaty fabrics in subtle shades. Likewise, a room where you wish to unwind needs soft filtered light, best achieved with fabrics such as linen or sheers, or textured blinds of rattan or bamboo. If your room needs to be more energising, you can use brightly coloured curtains and patterned blinds.

If you want to keep a view but protect your home's furnishings from the fading effect of ultraviolet rays, choose a sunscreen blind of PVC-coated fibreglass. Its open weave lets you see through the blind, especially if the fabric is in a darker colour. And for total privacy, it's still hard to beat venetian blinds.

1 *Glazed walls can be used to visually enlarge living areas. Artworks have been displayed along the side fence of this inner-city home to intensify the illusion of it being another interior wall. The integration of indoors and out is completed with a set of doors that slide back to connect the living room with the courtyard.*

2 *For those people lucky enough to have a waterfront home, an open-plan design such as this is ideal for the living area. Sunlight spills in all day through clerestory windows and skylights, and when the weather is balmy, panels in the wall on the water side are slid open, extending the living area to the terrace.*

Escape from daily life. Home theatre is re-creating the cinema experience from your

2

1 Halogen downlights fitted with dimmers let you dial down the light in a media room, taking it as close to a cinema experience as possible. This home theatre is set up in a formal living area. Along with the downlights for movie sessions, it has a backlit glass panel behind the television. This luminous fitting adds a deal of sophistication to the room when it's not in home-theatre mode.

2 Multi-purpose storage units make a chameleon of any living space, transforming it into a work, family or formal area, as necessary. The joinery on this unit contains the entertainment system, and conceals a wine cellar, glassware and a fold-out ironing board; it even has room for bicycles.

3 Technology has progressed a long way since 1887 when Thomas Edison first patented a motion picture camera. Today, many homes have a dedicated cinema room. This one was set up in the basement so other living areas would be free of home-theatre equipment. It has carpet on the floor and fabric on the walls to help with soundproofing.

3

own lounge chair

MEDIA ROOMS

1 A pile of cushions makes outdoor furniture both colourful and comfortable. The benches along this verandah are lined with cushions that are easily removed during wet weather. You should keep a box or trunk on the verandah to store the cushions, as even waterproof fabrics start to smell and decay when left out in the weather. Change covers regularly for a fresh look.

2 The side of a house is sometimes neglected as more focus seems to go on the front and backyards. This space can, however, be used as a private retreat, especially if it's off a main or guest bedroom. A narrow verandah on this villa-style home is the perfect spot for a breakfast table and two chairs.

3 Appeal to your sense of touch with textured paving underfoot. This tropical home invites a barefoot lifestyle with its blended indoor and outdoor spaces. Pathways of concrete pavers and pebbles join separate pavilions set around a feature pond. The finished effect is a smooth journey for the feet and an attraction for the eye.

4 Good things can come in small packages, as this compact home demonstrates. Instead of approaching the apartment balcony as a separate space, this design makes it an extension of the living area. The built-in seating nook means valuable floor space isn't taken up by outdoor chairs.

DECKS & VERANDAHS

Lazing on a verandah with a glass of wine brings on an instant holiday mood

EXTERIOR COLOURS

The exterior of your home should be in harmony with the surrounding streetscape, but it need not be devoid of individual style. Colour is probably the simplest way to mark out your home from those of your neighbours.

You can apply colour as paint or render to walls, or leave the bricks and timber in their existing hues. Roofing – tile or corrugated metal – and guttering are other places to bring in exterior colour. Remember, though, that a dark roof absorbs ultraviolet light (UV) and heat while a light-coloured material will reflect it. This transfer through the roof can account for up to 35 per cent of heat entering the house in summer.

Verandah posts, garden walls, lattice work or boundary fences can be painted to make a smooth connection between internal and external spaces. Make sure any paint you use on an exterior surface includes UV protectors to guard against chemical breakdown and fading. Just think of it as sunscreen for the walls. Some pigments are less resilient outdoors – red and blue are notorious fast-faders – although good-quality exterior paints should not have this problem.

While the history of a house should be respected in your colour choice, there is no need to slavishly follow a heritage scheme with Brunswick green and Indian red trim. The current trend is for putty and sandstone colours, trimmed with dark blue, teal green or charcoal. Outdoor feature walls, used in courtyards or to set off fountains and sculpture, have mellowed from the intense pinks, blues and oranges of a decade ago to softer 'muddied-up' hues of slate blue, terracotta and aubergine.

The fashion in brick is for natural tones and bricks that are not overly textured. Lighter colours are preferred in Australia's northern areas, while in the south more reds and browns are being used. Some architect-designed houses are being constructed of smooth-faced brick in matt tones of olive through to dark brown and charcoal.

Remember, when exterior walls are painted in dark colours, it can make a house recede and seem to diminish in size. A light finish, on the other hand, will make it seem larger, and red tones always advance, so features appear more prominent.

1 *You'll feel as though you're permanently on holiday in a home that's set up for lazing in the sun. With no shortage of sun chairs or outdoor decks, this house makes relaxation a high priority. For the ultimate holiday at home, string up a hammock, pour a cocktail and simply relax.*

2 *Matching your outdoor furniture to the style of the deck creates visual harmony. The contemporary lines of this house are echoed in the sleek design of the deck chairs.*

3 *This patio taps into the trend for having outdoor rooms instead of gardens. It's the furniture that gives this space its character. A retractable sunscreen shelters the 'room' so it can remain set up in all conditions.*

4 *With its distinct Mediterranean feel, this verandah is worlds away from the bustle of daily life. A lush sprawl of ivy on the wall makes the back garden seem more intimate.*

4

Find a spot to sit yourself in the sun. Outdoor areas can be just as much sanctuaries

as any room indoors

CANDLE MAKING

YOU'LL NEED

- moulds suitable for candle-making (Metal and heat-resistant plastic are best, but glazed china or pottery moulds are also suitable. Ensure the base of the mould is narrower than the top, to allow the candles to be removed from the moulds.)
- petroleum jelly
- wick and metal wick sinkers
- bamboo skewers (about 15cm long)
- adhesive tape
- newspapers
- candle wax
- saucepan and ladle
- beads with large holes (optional), to use for trims if desired

METHOD

1 Smear the inside of the moulds with petroleum jelly. Cut a generous length of wick and attach a wick sinker to one end. Place the wick sinker at the base of the mould. Wind the other end of the wick around a bamboo skewer until the wick is taut in the middle of the mould. Lie the skewer across the top of mould and secure with adhesive tape.

2 Place the moulds on top of several layers of newspaper in a place where they can remain undisturbed for a few hours. The newspaper protects the surface of your bench from the heat of the wax and helps soak up spills.

3 Melt the wax in a saucepan over a slow heat. Never allow the wax to boil and remove it from the heat if it begins to smoke. (Always have a secure-fitting lid nearby in case of fire.) When the wax is melted, either pour it into the mould from the saucepan or use a ladle to quickly spoon it in.

4 Leave the candles to set without moving them for at least two hours.

5 Leave the candles to harden for 24 hours before removing from the moulds.

6 To remove a candle from the mould, sit the mould in a container of near-boiling water, with the water level equal to the top of the wax inside. When the wax begins to melt around the sides, remove the mould.

MAKE IT @ HOME

For indoors and outside, candles create a soft mood that gives a sense of wellbeing

HOME MOVIES

HINT *Be a ruthless editor. And don't worry about deleting too much; the footage will still stay on the digital video camera's memory until you record over it.*

YOU'LL NEED

- digital video camera (FireWire or iLink compatible)
- Apple Mac loaded with iMovie (free with iLife on all new Macs) or a PC with Microsoft Movie Maker 2 (free with Windows XP)
- FireWire or iLink cable (IEEE 1394 cable) to connect camera to computer
- IEEE 1394 card (standard on all new Macs and PCs, but you may need one fitted if you have an older computer)
- to make a DVD, you'll need a DVD burner and a program such as iDVD for Macs (also free with iLife) or Sonic MyDVD 5 for PCs
- lots of memory space on your computer's hard drive

METHOD

1. Decide on a theme or concept for your home movie. It can be a record of your travels or a special occasion, or an epic adventure. Draft a script or running sheet to help you stay focused and cut editing time.

2. Using a digital video camera, start filming or take some photos with a digital camera to also splice into the movie.

3. Plug your camera into a computer, using a FireWire or iLink cable (IEEE 1394 cable), then switch your camera to VCR or VTR mode.

4. Importing your footage is now as simple as a click of the mouse. Both iMovie and Microsoft Movie Maker 2 have tutorials and online help. Visit www.apple.com.au/ilife/imovie/ or www.microsoft.com/windowsxp/using/moviemaker/videos/create.mspx

5. Once you have imported the footage, both programs will detect scene breaks and separate the footage into clips. With a thumbnail of each clip, you can edit away, dragging and dropping each into a timeline.

6. Once you have the basic scene sequence, you may add music, special effects, titles, transitions and voice-overs. Beginners may like to stick to the software's library of sounds but you can also import from many different music/sound programs such as iGarage or Sound Forge.

7. Burn your movie to DVD. Apple's iMovie works in conjunction with iDVD so you will only need an internal/external burner. PC users will need to buy additional software such as Sonic MyDVD 5.

8. Once your masterpiece is complete, choose an evening to sit back, munch popcorn and enjoy the show.

MAKE IT @ HOME

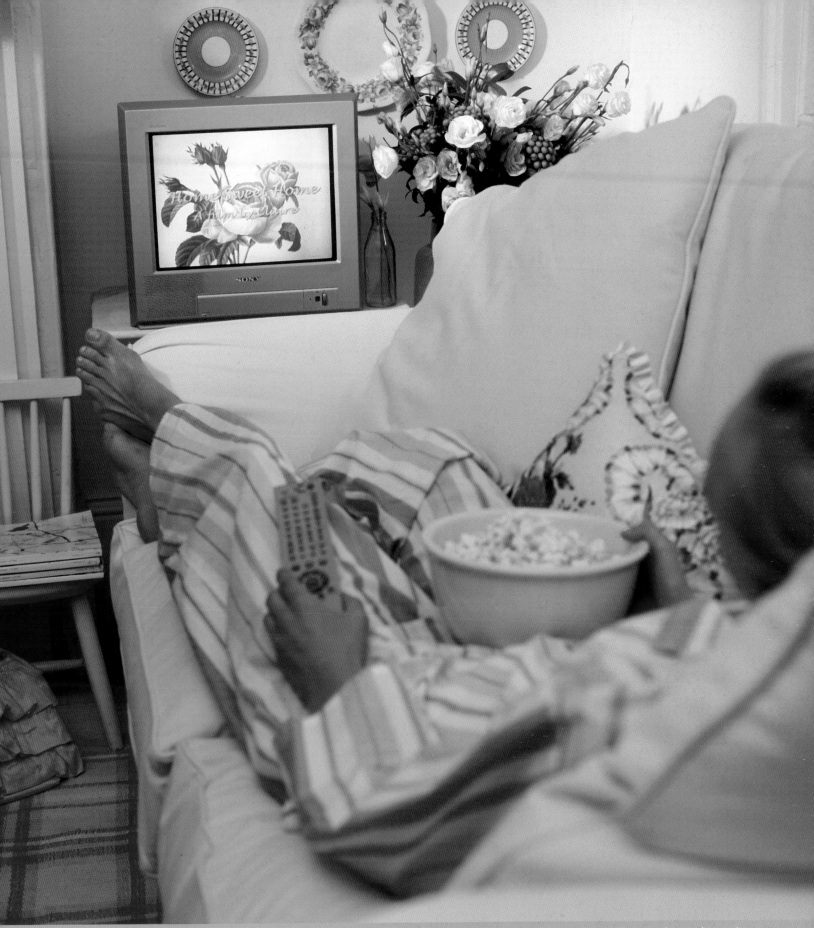

Capture memories forever. Home movies have been reinvigorated by digital technology

REFLECT & RELEASE

Sliding into a deep warm bath (bubbles optional) is a simple recipe for relaxation that has been soothing souls since ancient times. ~ Increasingly, the home bathroom is being turned into a retreat. It's a place where you can pamper your body and, at the same time, let your mind wander from the cares of a busy day. ~ But soothing tension is not always about being passive. Exercise is a brilliant way of releasing stress and lifting your mood, and having a place where you can work out or practise yoga will inspire you to keep moving. That feeling of stillness you can achieve after an exercise session is as beneficial for your spirit as the physical activity is for your muscles. ~ Making a home where you can be reflective means catering to your body as well as your mind. Your sanctuary is a place to delight the senses, not deny them.

It's simple to refocus your energy at the end of the day with some fragrant bubbles

1 *While the ensuite is sometimes considered the little sister to the main bathroom, this one proves that big is beautiful. You can lavish the best finishes, designer tapware and a deep bath on this most personal of rooms, This bath, set into a timber base, promises a relaxing soak away from everyday annoyances.*

2 *A grand arch gives an alluring Romanesque touch to this bathroom, and the soothing effect of the restful colours is enhanced with the fragrance of lavender. Scented candles in rose and jasmine will give a sensual element to your bathing experience, as will adding essential oils to your bath.*

previous page
What a great place to unwind at the end of the day. Filtered sunlight and an all-white decor ensure this is the place to go when you need a little inspiration.

and heated towels

BATHROOMS

PLANNING A RELAXING BATHROOM

Deep baths, massaging showers, finely fragranced toiletries and soft warm towels turn a bathroom into an indulgent retreat. Practicality is still paramount, of course, but a few beautiful inclusions can make all the difference. King François I of France hung Leonardo da Vinci's portrait 'Mona Lisa' in his royal bathroom, but you need not be that extravagant. Think of the bathroom vanity and cupboards more as pieces of furniture and choose a style that particularly appeals to you. If you have the space, you could include an armoire, a table or an upholstered chair, but make sure any timber is sealed with at least three coats of polyurethane and that fabrics are waterproofed.

Keeping the room's temperature comfortable is essential, too. A temperature of 22 °C lets you avoid the shivers. Underfloor heating is expensive, but the pleasure of warm tiles under bare feet may well justify the cost. A less pricey option is an all-in-one overhead light, fan and heater unit, or a fan-assisted ceramic heater. A heated towel rail, with its promise of warm, dry towels, is another welcome indulgence.

Central to relaxation in your bathroom is the bath – the deeper the better. An unhurried soak helps release tense muscles, and listening to music while you're in the bath adds to the pleasure. You can enjoy some aromatherapy by adding a few drops of essential oils to the tub or an oil-burner; jasmine, neroli and ylang-ylang are said to be deeply relaxing. A colour scheme of soft greens, blues, silver or neutrals also brings a sense of calm as you bathe by slowing your heartbeat and lowering your blood pressure.

A shower can be therapeutic, too, especially if your shower's spray can be set to a pulsing massage. You'll be surprised at how your entire bathing experience can be improved simply by investing in a new showerhead.

Try to continue that quiet, unstressed feeling once you step out of the shower or bath. An explosion of clutter can really distract from a relaxing experience, so display only a few pampering products and keep the remainder stored within a wet arm's reach. Remember, good storage is the key to serenity. An abundance of rolled or stacked towels is another easy extravagance. Be generous – you really do need two towels!

Lighting should be soft to complement the mood. Having a light fitted with a dimmer switch or placing candles around the room gives a more appealing effect than the single overhead fluorescent bulb. But don't forget – you need good, even lighting around the bathroom mirror for applying make-up or shaving.

Essentially, your bathroom plan can be as involved as your budget allows. Calming colours, a heater and subdued lighting won't break the bank but they will give the room softness, so that you enjoy closing the bathroom door and simply relaxing.

1 Bring glamour to the space with one beautiful feature. An antique Venetian mirror in this bathroom stands out against the contemporary scheme. Walls and floors are tiled in honed limestone. Added lustre could also come from a chandelier or crystal candle-holders.

2 Muted greens inspire a restful atmosphere. In this attic area, mossy green weatherboards frame a dormer window. Having the bathroom in the attic means the room is always warm; plantation shutters on the window admit breezes.

3 Bathing takes on a new dimension when it's shared with someone special. The generous spa bath here has plenty of room for two. Glass bricks and a skylight let in the sunshine but retain privacy. Glass bricks are also good insulators and will keep the heat in during winter, saving you money on your energy bill.

allowing you to relax both mind and body

1 *Timber gives this room a warm and sophisticated feel. The wall panels turn it into an elegant suite and somewhat disguise the room's function as a place for washing. Any timber should be finished with a waterproof sealant and restricted to drier areas of the room. Here, mosaics are used in the wetter bath and shower areas.*

2 *Art need not be forgotten in the bathroom. A sculptural artwork, seen through a glass-panelled wall, is the focal point of this modern scheme. While paintings and fabric can become damp and mouldy in this humid environment, sealed timber or metal sculptures are ideal.*

Water refreshes body and soul, whether you simply dip your toe or float away and

1 Stepping stones appear to float above the water of this pool. The concrete steppers lead your eye into the adjacent living areas, where concertina doors can be folded back. Walking 'on' the pool rather than beside it brings the calming effect of the rippling water even closer.

2 Part of an urban sanctuary, this Zen-like pool area is ideal for yoga or a cooling plunge. White concrete walls are teamed with timber decking for a clean, fresh look. The divide between a home's interior and the outside is blurred by the use of a similar colour scheme and having expanses of glass.

forget yourself

SWIMMING POOLS

WATER THERAPY

You've been bombarded with the message that drinking eight glasses of water a day is essential for your health. But you don't have to swallow the stuff to feel its benefits: water does just as much good to the soul as the body.

Just think how calming it is to be near the sea. You may not be fortunate enough to be lulled to sleep by the rhythmic sound of waves at night, but the trickle of a backyard water feature can have a similarly calming effect. And there's a reason why dentists' waiting rooms have a tropical fishtank on one wall – anything to relax the patients.

Maybe it has to do with 60 per cent of the adult human body being water that something like a swimming pool in the garden is such a magnetic, refreshing oasis. It's a place not only for exercise, but also for rest and relaxation, and a focal point for alfresco entertaining. Even if you don't have room for a full-sized pool, an outdoor spa can give you yet another way of unwinding.

As for water indoors, the bathroom is becoming one of the most important rooms in the house. As you relax in the tub it's not hard to understand why bathing is considered a spiritual experience in Japanese culture. The steam room also has importance in Native American and Scandinavian traditions. Simple showers have been discovered in ancient Egyptian ruins, and the Romans made public bathhouses as sociable as bars or restaurants are today.

Some Roman emperors are said to have bathed seven or eight times a day. Spending that sort of time bathing is unheard of these days (not to mention impossible with water restrictions), but that shouldn't stop you making the most of whatever moments you can snatch from your busy schedule. That could mean setting up candles around the bathroom, putting on your favourite soothing CD and using bubble bath, bath essence or a few drops of your chosen essential oil. You'll be surprised how quickly the stresses of the day will wash away and aching muscles are soothed.

Showers can be as relaxing as baths. Simply using a body wash infused with either peppermint or eucalyptus will ease muscular aches and lift a tired mood. Don't skimp on bathing accessories, either – loofahs, sponges, bathmitts and other items cost virtually nothing, but can upgrade a daily habit to an indulgence.

For those inclined towards having a good steam, there's always the option of installing your own steam room. The Finns called their steam saunas 'the medicine of the poor'. Everyone knows how well steam soothes irritated airways and relieves congestion when you have a cold, but the warmth of a steam bath also relaxes stiff muscles and stimulates blood circulation to the skin. Even if you lack the space for a steam room, just breathing in the moist warm air that comes with a shower can clear your head and give your skin a healthy glow. Enjoying a steam may or may not cleanse your spirit, but it's definitely a bonus for the weary body.

Sunlight playing on the surface of a pool is every bit as calming as the sound of

3

1 Exercise in style in an executive-style lap pool. Swimming is a great cardiovascular work-out that increases blood circulation and tones the whole body. Swimming causes less stress on the body than running, and taking the plunge is easy when a pool is so close at hand.

2 An unobtrusive glass fence keeps this pool safe and secure without interfering with the view. The barrier contains the splashes, but still allows through the ripples of light that reflect off the water's surface.

3 Water nudges this living area, with a pool on one side and a garden pond on the other. The sight and sound of falling water is calming, and here a curtain of water flows into a plunge pool. For the ultimate in water massage, position spa jets at graduating heights around the pool to set up a circuit.

water splashing from a fountain

PLANNING FOR FITNESS

Exercise is good for you, no matter your age. It really is a case of use it or lose it: researchers have found that at least half the physical decline associated with ageing is brought on by inactivity rather than by the ageing process itself.

Regular exercise strengthens the heart and other muscles and reduces blood pressure. Aerobic activity increases lung capacity and weight-bearing exercise helps keep bones strong. Overall, regular exercise helps you maintain good balance and avoid falls.

Creating an achievable fitness plan is a great first step towards enjoying a fit, healthy lifestyle. Set yourself realistic goals in the short, middle and long term. Write down the goals, how you wish to achieve each one and then set yourself a deadline. Leave a space to track and measure your progress or try keeping an exercise diary for the first three months to really find your rhythm.

Discovering the best exercise for you may take time. Before committing to a gym or a team sport, consider a trial period. At the same time, start taking regular walks and slowly increase your distance. You could also have a few sessions with an exercise professional to work out a suitable fitness routine for you. Remember that a variety of activities is more beneficial as it exercises different muscles and joints. Doing your exercise sessions with a friend is a good way to keep motivated.

Always warm up with gentle stretches and activity before you exercise and warm down thoroughly, too. This reduces the risk of soft tissue injuries, sprains and strains.

Start off slowly and aim for small improvements. You may not see a huge difference straight away, but don't be discouraged – increased flexibility, endurance, better sleeping and general wellbeing are all benefits of improved fitness. Add a balanced diet to your daily schedule and you're well on your way to good health.

HOW MUCH EXERCISE?

To maintain good health, it's recommended you do at least 30 minutes of moderate physical activity on all days. It doesn't have to be continuous; you can do three sessions of around 10 to 15 minutes. Activities could be brisk walking, mowing the lawn, digging in the garden, or medium-paced swimming or cycling.

If you want to improve your fitness levels, you need to do more – 30 minutes of continuous vigorous exercise on three or four days each week, as well as the recommended amount of moderate activity. Vigorous exercise makes you huff and puff. Technically, it's exercising where your heart rate reaches 70-85 per cent of the maximum heart rate (calculated at 220 minus your age). It's achieved with brisk walking, active sports such as football and netball, jogging, speed walking, aerobics and circuit training. Consult a doctor before starting on a vigorous exercise program if you haven't exercised for some years, if you have a health problem or have relatives with heart disease. Pregnant women should avoid vigorous exercise.

For many people, swimming laps becomes a sort of meditation that helps them

1 An abundance of plants can turn a lap pool into a tropical haven. Palm trees, bird-of-paradise (Strelitzia), agapanthus and viburnum give a lush, island feel. Shade shouldn't be forgotten either. Here, a canvas shade extends from the house. You could also stretch a sail-shade over the water.

2 You don't need to swim to benefit from water's rejuvenating properties. A small pond, such as this Balinese-style design, can be a central point of relaxation in the home. Add plants such as lilies or dwarf papyrus and a few fish.

3 Surrounded by natural bushland, this elevated lap pool is the height of eco-resort style. The colours and natural textures of stone and timber blend with the bush surrounds. Rather than cutting down trees, you could shape your pool around them. It may mean cleaning out more leaves, but the closeness to nature should compensate.

4 The living is easy with a shaded entertaining area. A stepped, Japanese-inspired pool makes things seem even cooler with the sound of its trickling water. Louvred ceiling panels block harsh sunlight and direct the airflow. With skin cancer such a problem, a shaded outdoor retreat is the sun-smart way to go.

unwind after a busy day

1 *Free yourself of inhibitions in a day spa that connects with the outdoors. White river pebbles and steppers stretch from the private garden and under an outdoor shower to the bathroom inside. A sandstone wall provides privacy without restricting the feeling of freedom.*

2 *It's not only the sight and feel of water that pacifies but also its gentle sound. Get your day spa in tune with nature by introducing a gentle flow of water. The water feature in this atrium creates a soothing sound that can be heard throughout the home.*

Opening your private rooms to the sun and air breathes life into your whole being

THE ART OF MASSAGE

Life can be stressful, especially if you've had a bad week at work or been running around after the kids. Often when you're stressed, that tension transfers to your muscles. Getting a stiff neck and shoulders is common, and a lot of people also hold tension in their arms and backsides. It might seem indulgent, but a massage could be just what you need. Massaging these muscles 'unknots' them, allowing the body to relax.

You don't need regular sessions with a trained masseuse to benefit. Some techniques are so simple you and a friend could easily give and receive massages at home.

The best time to have a massage is just before bedtime (for a good night's sleep), and the best place is on the floor or on a bed – but even the kitchen table will do. To make the surface more comfortable, cushion it with a mat or some towels. It's important that the masseuse is in a comfortable position, too, or it could lead to back strain.

Make the room relaxing by playing soothing music and adding calming essential oils such as sandalwood, lavender or ylang-ylang to an oil-burner. Dim the lights or use candles to create a soft glow. If the room is cool, put on a heater. Put towels in the dryer and use them to keep those parts of the body not being massaged warm.

Massage is easy to do but go gently – massaging incorrectly can cause problems. The basis of a simple, relaxing massage is the effleurage movement. Effleurage involves using both hands laid flat and applying pressure in long strokes towards the heart. When you have finished the 'up' stroke, release the pressure and run your hands back down, but don't take your hands off the person being massaged. Using a massage oil, either almond or grapeseed, makes it easier to glide over the muscles.

Before you begin, 'warm up' the person you are massaging. Have them lie face down, then lightly rub their back, shoulders and neck to get the blood flowing. Next, massage their back using effleurage. Have them turn over, then massage the upper muscles that connect the shoulders to the neck. Make your hands into fists and place them under the shoulders. Using light pressure, move your fists in circular movements.

On the neck itself, support your 'client's' head with one hand while gently using the effleurage movement on one side, then swap sides (but always support the head). Gently turn their head and, using only your fingertips, lightly massage the muscles along the side of the neck. Never force the movement.

Finally, using your fingertips, massage the scalp with rhythmic, circular movements, then relieve any tension in the face by gently massaging the temples. Finish with a warm-down of simple light rubbing.

The human touch is wonderful therapy and learning to massage allows you to share the gift of relaxation with your loved ones. If you'd like to find out more about massage techniques, you could look at some of the many books available on massage, or do a short course at a community college. Happiness could lie in your hands.

Look forward to coming home by creating an atmosphere in which you can unwind

1 A bath with a view is the height of day-spa luxury. Dreaming comes easily when you have a vista to inspire you while you have a long, relaxing soak. Choose tones and textures that blend with the materials used in the outdoor area, and windows or doors that open wide to let in the breezes.

2 Togetherness is encouraged in this bathroom retreat. Its wonderfully large shower area is roomy enough for two to bathe at the same time. A double-basin vanity and double towel rails also confirm that two are welcome.

3 You want to create an atmosphere in which you can unwind, exhale and breathe. Fresh air is a constant feature of this room, thanks to a panel of louvres and glass sliding door. Keep a window open and try breathing techniques for meditation and relaxation.

4 Borrowing the glamour of a five-star resort gives your home that indulgent day-spa vibe. Opening this bedroom to a private spa-pool area sets a scene for pampering. Having water so close to the sleeping zone will aid in relaxation, too. Add greenery for the perfect urban oasis.

and breathe. Just being still can be a luxury

1 *A home sauna delivers the health benefits of heat. The increased temperature stimulates blood circulation, bringing more nutrients to the skin and other organs. Heat also eases any muscular aches after exercise. In a sauna, you pour water on hot stones to produce steam. Adding a little eucalyptus oil to the water can help ease sinus problems and aid in breathing. After the sauna, take a shower to wash off toxins that have been sweated out of your system.*

2 *The great outdoors is the perfect backdrop for exercise. Clean air and cool breezes makes things pleasant, and the landscape can be an interesting distraction. This verandah work-out area combines the privacy and comfort of home with the tranquillity of nature. Store equipment indoors, however, to prevent it from rusting.*

3 *Weight training increases strength, flexibility and your general wellbeing. By creating sets of repetitious lifts, you can strengthen the various muscle groups. Experts advise lifting weights at least three times a week. Making the effort is easier when you have a home gym that is full of light and air, and with a gentle garden outlook.*

CREATING AN EXERCISE ROOM

It can be hard to find time for exercise in a busy life, so having a place where you can work out at home is an attractive option. There is no travelling to and from the gym and, once you're set up, no expensive gym fees.

The home gym can be as simple or as complex as you like, from a skipping rope and dumb-bells to multistations and step machines. What is most important is that it's a place you want to go. Choose an area with natural light, where you can open a window for fresh air. Try to ensure it's a place that doesn't get too hot or cold – an ambient temperature from 18 to 22°C is most comfortable.

If you want to have gym equipment like a treadmill or multistation, make sure the floor can take the weight. The room will need a ceiling height of at least 2.4 metres and there should also be enough space for you to move easily around any machines. You should lay down rubber matting to protect the floor and provide sound insulation.

Boredom is the biggest problem when it comes to exercising regularly, so try to create a space that you associate with fun, rather than seeing exercising as a chore. Add splashes of vibrant orange or red to speed up your pulse rate and lift your spirits. Including a stereo system, a television or just a view out the window in a home gym can also make you more inclined to go and work out.

HOME GYMS

Gear up for the day ahead with a visit to your home gym

HEALTHY JUICES

Fruit and vegetables are essential to a healthy diet, and a glass of freshly squeezed juice is an easy way to grab all that goodness. Having been extracted from raw fruit and vegetables, juices are particularly good sources of vitamins A, C and E and enzymes that aid digestion. The high water content in juice also means vitamins are easily absorbed by your body. But don't replace eating your fruit and vegies with drinking juice; dietary fibre is also needed for good health.

To make your juice, use ripe fruit and vegetables, and the freshest you can find, as these will have more vitamins. If you choose organically grown produce, they can be scrubbed rather than peeled before juicing, keeping more of the nutrients which are found just under the skin.

Make sure that your juicer is clean – you don't want added mould in the mix. Trim, peel or scrub your produce, then cut it into sizes suitable for your juicer. Process each type of fruit and vegie on its own, rather than a mix of, say, apple and orange pieces, so the juicer works effectively, then combine the resulting juices. Drink it as soon as you can; exposure to the air causes oxidisation which breaks down nutrients and gives juice a sour taste.

To make a smoothie, blend juices with banana, soy milk or yoghurt. Parsnip juice also gives sweet creaminess to a blend.

The concentrated juices of any fruit and vegetables are good for you but don't overdo it – a glass of juice can be potent stuff. Dark green juices, such as spinach and watercress, and dark red juices like beetroot are too strong to drink alone. Dilute them with apple or celery juice or water. The high sugar content in fresh fruit juice can also aggravate gastritis and other bowel disorders and can be a problem for diabetics. Even if you have good digestion, three average glasses of juice a day is probably enough.

Finding your favourite juice blend will mean mixing, matching and experimenting. To start, juice the ingredients separately and then blend.

SUGGESTED JUICE COMBINATIONS

Smooth fruit blend: banana, orange and strawberries

Hangover healers (your body will love the vitamin C and betacarotene): pineapple and mango; or apple, carrot and wheatgrass

Berry delight: pineapple, apple, blueberries, strawberries and raspberries

Immune defence (big on vitamin C and betacarotene): apple, carrot, ginger and orange

Super cleanser (traditionally, Russians believe that beetroot cleanses the blood): carrot, apple, beetroot, spinach and cucumber

MAKE IT @ HOME

Looking after your health and wellbeing is essential, so pour yourself a fresh juice daily

BLENDING ESSENTIAL OILS

Fragrance has a powerful effect on your mood. The part of your brain that processes smell is associated with the limbic system, your body's emotional switchboard. Aromatherapy uses essential oils from plants to affect your emotional and physical state. Different oils have different properties: some are relaxing, others invigorating. By blending the oils, aromatherapists tailor their treatments to relieve specific symptoms.

Essential oils may be used in a massage, in a bath or an oil-burner. For massage, essential oils are diluted in a carrier oil such as sweet almond or grapeseed to avoid irritating the skin. The recommended proportion is five drops of essential oil to 10ml of carrier oil. Test the mix on a small section of skin before you use it and if irritation occurs, add more carrier oil.

Pre-blended oils don't have the flexibility of homemade blends, and by making up smaller quantities, you avoid wasting often expensive essential oils. Use an eye-dropper for exact proportions, and store massage oil in a glass container in the fridge until shortly before use.

SUGGESTED BLENDS

Relaxing blend: 4 drops patchouli, 2 drops orange, 2 drops sandalwood

Uplifting blend: 5 drops bergamot, 2 drops orange, 1 drop ylang ylang

Calming blend: 3 drops marjoram, 2 drops lavender, 2 drops sandalwood

Stimulating blend: 3 drops rosemary, 2 drops lemon, 3 drops pine

Balancing blend: 2 drops geranium, 3 drops lavender, 2 drops cedarwood

WARNING

Pregnant women should avoid using all essential oils during the first trimester, and consult a health professional before using any essential oils in later pregnancy. You should also consult a qualified aromatherapist before using essential oils on children or people with conditions such as high blood pressure or epilepsy. Essential oils must never be taken internally.

MAKE IT @ HOME

Scent has a powerful effect on your body; use it to uplift or to calm and relax

REST & RELAX

You're most at peace in those gentle moments just
before sleep descends. Snuggling into a familiar bed
at night is a comforting experience. Waking in
a serene, sun-filled space is just as pleasurable,
and having a morning cuppa in bed must be one of
the gentlest ways to start the day. ~ Your bedroom
is a place of sleep, intimacy, dreams and rest. It's
an intensely personal room, so create a nurturing
environment for yourself. ~ But personal retreats
are not confined to the bedroom. Think where
else you can create a pocket of calm; perhaps it's
a sunny nook in the kitchen or a favourite chair in
the living room. Any zone dedicated to unwinding
should be clear of clutter and suffused with a soft
light to enhance your sense of contentment. Close
your eyes and breathe deep ... it's time to rest.

1 This bedroom is a calm composition of natural textures. Timber shutters open to a private garden with an abundance of plants. In such a laid-back atmosphere, order comes second to relaxation, and bedside essentials are casually combined on a raw timber table.

2 Sheer drops give a dreamy softness to this bedroom. Their fine fabric contrasts with the deep pinks of the bedlinen and damask-covered chair, and also gently filters the light in this sunny room. The effect is intensely romantic.

previous page
Make breakfast in bed a regular treat for yourself and someone special. There's no better place to be than snuggled beneath a warm quilt with a cup of tea. Feel totally spoiled.

The recipe for a good night's sleep is a calm mind, a relaxed body and a comfy bed

THE IMPORTANCE OF LIGHT

Natural light in the home can improve your mood, health and connection with the cycles of the day and night. Sunlight encourages your body to produce serotonin and dopamine – chemicals that stimulate the pleasure centre of the brain. The sun also supplies your daily dose of vitamin D (good for bone development). It's something to think about when you're deciding whether to lift the blinds or leave them shut.

Conversely, a lack of sunshine can reduce enthusiasm and make you listless, anxious or depressed. Known as seasonal affective disorder, or SAD syndrome, this condition is widely recognised in the northern hemisphere, where winters are long with little daylight. Even in Australia, which is spoilt for sunshine, you can experience a similar 'SADness' after only a few successive overcast days.

As well as brightening your mood, maximising natural light in your home can also reduce the need for lighting and heating. Warmth from the sun during the day is stored in walls, floors and furnishings and is radiated back as the temperature drops.

The amount of natural light a room receives is determined by its orientation. It's not possible for every room to face north – the most desirable aspect because it affords sun all day – so rooms are generally positioned according to their function.

Living spaces are active areas used by everyone, so they should be positioned to face north, if possible. East-facing rooms catch the morning sun – an ideal orientation for bedrooms and breakfast rooms. West-facing rooms get the afternoon sun – great in winter but you'll need blinds or curtains to temper summer heat. Living rooms can work well with a westerly aspect provided the decor visually warms the space in the morning and you have window coverings to beat the afternoon glare.

South-facing rooms tend to have a constant cool light, with no glare, but no shadows either. Bedrooms, bathrooms and utility rooms are the easiest to position here because they are more restful spaces. The stillness of a southerly aspect is least suitable for a study, home office or children's room – anywhere that creative energy needs to be at work. If these rooms do face south, warm them with bright colours.

The colour of the walls is important, too. White walls reflect 60-80 per cent of the light, amplifying its effect. Darker walls absorb light. To avoid glare in rooms bathed in sunshine, use softer hues like buttermilk or twine on walls rather than crisp white.

Yet as much as you need the light, you need the stillness of shadows, too – a respite for the imagination to wander its own way undazzled by distraction. Shadows are to sunlight what yin is to yang – complementary opposites, one enhancing the other.

Natural light in the home connects you with the cycles of day and night

1 The romance of the French provincial style gains a contemporary sophistication in this bedroom. Its charm lies in the simple layering of white on white, but choosing whites that complement each other takes skill. Fabrics in soft milk tones are best matched with furniture in more rustic whites to create a feeling of warmth.

2 A child's bedroom should suit play as well as rest. In this little girl's bedroom, walls are painted in a rich red and the decor is a charming mix of reclaimed furniture and fresh floral prints. The weathered tea chest was picked up at auction and relined with a Victorian-style fabric. Antique hat boxes, jewellery cases or rustic crates could also be revived in the same manner.

3 Colour, texture, action ... that's what it's all about in a room dedicated to children. And here you have it all, with a bedspread patterned in primary colours, textured pillowcases, easy-to-access cane-basket drawers and white walls for contrast. It's stimulating and fun – just what a little girl ordered.

4 A window seat is a wonderful inclusion in any bedroom. This one is made more private with floaty sheer curtains, while blinds are used to shut out the sun. Inviting quiet contemplation, a window seat takes up little space and can change the dynamic of the bedroom from merely a place of sleep to a personal sanctuary.

1

1 A suede chaise longue makes the most of the generous space in this room. The sunniest spot in any bedroom can become a corner for reading or just relaxing with a daybed, armchair or comfortable sofa. This caramel chaise blends in well with the earthy hues and timbers of this sophisticated scheme.

2 The circular window seems to emphasise the simplicity of this bedroom. It is made even more of a feature by painting the wall in a contrasting colour. Having just the one strong feature in a room, and muting other elements so it remains the focus, can create an atmosphere of serenity.

3 This minimalist bedroom capitalises on space and sleek design. The large bedside tables swallow clutter, leaving their tops clear to show off a pair of geometric lamps. The dark colour scheme helps subdue the light coming in from outside, so that the room remains restful.

4 Bring the elegance of a five-star hotel to your own bedroom with handsome prints and customised furnishings. The beautiful coordination of fabrics, a key to the hotel style, can inspire relaxation. In this room a custom-made bedhead and cushions are matched with tailored bedding. Their softness contrasts with the shine of the mirrored tables.

1 A false wall painted in vibrant red conceals the clothes storage behind. It streamlines the look of the room as it removes the need for a bulky wardrobe. Wicker chairs serve a double function as seats and bedside tables.

2 Midnight blue gives intimacy to this bedroom. The deep hue is partnered with red carpet and warm coloured timber. Teaming similar tones of blue and red can look surprisingly harmonious – remember that together they create the deep purples of twilight. If you want to add drama to large spaces, be adventurous with cobalt, navy or sapphire.

CHOOSING BEDLINEN

You spend, on average, 24 years of your life in bed, so make it as pleasant as you can. Dress your bed in fine cotton sheets with a thread count of at least 180 per square inch (standard sheets have a thread count of 150). Sheets with a higher thread count are woven from finer fibres, so are softer and more resistant to pilling. Those made from Egyptian or pima cotton are considered to be the best, as these varieties have extra-long fibres that produce finer threads and the smoothest, most long-lasting fabrics.

Choose natural fibres for blankets and quilts, too. Unlike acrylic, which can leave you feeling overheated and clammy, wool or cotton blankets adapt better to changes in temperature and humidity, letting your body breathe while you slumber. And a woollen underlay brings immediate softness to a bed, quickly lulling you to sleep.

A fluffed-up quilt looks the ultimate in cosiness, but may be too warm for the average Australian winter. Quilts with synthetic fillings are especially notorious for hotting things up, resulting in a disturbed sleep. While they are weightier, a couple of blankets can be easily pulled up or left off to suit the temperature.

When it comes to choosing colours and styles, be inspired by the sensual nature of a bedroom. Make a sanctuary in soothing tones and dreamy colours, and lavish your bed with cushions and soft throws to create an inviting nest.

The bedroom is the place to indulge your own tastes. It's the place you see last

thing at night and first thing in the morning

IMPORTANCE OF SLEEP

Sleep rejuvenates both your body and mind. Getting enough of it is as vital for good health as a balanced diet and regular exercise. For most people seven to eight hours of sleep each night is best, but children and adolescents require at least nine hours.

Researchers believe sleep gives neurons a chance to shut down and repair themselves. Parts of the brain associated with emotions and social interaction show much reduced activity during deep sleep, and this downtime may be needed to fuel social activity when you're awake. There's also evidence that during sleep the brain repeats patterns of activity generated during the day, helping in learning and encoding memories.

While you snooze, cells in your body increase their production of proteins essential for cell growth and repair. And during deep sleep, the growth hormone is released in children and young adults – they *do* need their sleep to grow big and strong.

In 1964, university student Randy Gardner went 11 days without sleep and suffered no lasting ill-effects, but for most people it would be a different story. Lose out on sleep and your concentration suffers. Chronic sleep deprivation makes it hard to think straight and can lead to emotional disturbances. It also affects the functioning of your thyroid, causes secretion of the stress hormone, cortisol, and impairs your immune system.

In a busy life, often the first thing to be rationed is sleep. Even when there is time to have a rest, you might not be able to switch off. To train yourself into snoozing, associate the bed only with rest. Remove distractions like the television and only go to bed when you are tired. Even reading in bed can interfere with getting to sleep.

Avoid eating a big meal within the two hours before you go to bed. Your body shouldn't be put to work when you are ready to rest. And don't have caffeine or excessive sugar after 4pm: they are stimulants that will keep you awake.

To feel more rested, try taking a bath before bed. It's actually the drop in temperature after you get out of the warm water that makes you feel drowsy. Add essential oils such as chamomile, lavender or bergamot to the water or on your pillow.

Regular exercise is important, but try to finish any vigorous work-outs at least three hours before you plan to go to sleep. The endorphins your body produces during exercise create a natural high that's more conducive to waking up than snoozing.

You'll also aid sleep by creating a calm atmosphere in the bedroom. Keep it clutter-free and decorate it with restful colours like light blues, pale purples and greens.

When it comes to choosing a style, be inspired by the bedroom's sensual nature.

2

3

1 An elaborate four-poster bed, dressed in crisp white with a tantalising faux-fur throw, looks fit for a king. The other colours in the room are subtle so that the bed, although large, does not overpower the space.

2 Faux fur and big pillows give a decidedly decadent look to this otherwise tailored bed. Lined with satin, the faux-fur throw is silky to the touch and a perfect winter cover-up when you're reading or taking an afternoon nap. It can also be less mess and fuss than a mohair throw.

3 The bedroom is your private domain, and for some people that means pure indulgence. This opulent room feeds the senses with sumptuous fabrics, French gilding and a trompe l'oeil canopy and bedhead. Piles of plump cushions and a luscious quilt make this room a cosy nest.

This is the place for opulent silks, sumptuous faux fur and piles of cushions

The ensuite is an extension of the bedroom, providing a welcoming inner sanctum

1 *This open-plan bedroom and ensuite puts romance high on the agenda. A deep spa bath acts as a low room divider. As it is part of the bedroom, there is also space for a chair and stool, ready for discarded clothes or to be used as a seat for someone enjoying a facial treatment.*

2 *The water view beyond the balcony of this parents' retreat would soothe anyone's jangled nerves. A bath with a view is a place to revive the spirit. It doesn't have to be a fabulous water view; a pretty garden scene would be just as calming. The feeling of space and serenity in this ensuite is emphasised by a subtle scheme of creamy latte and chocolate tones, and the expanses of glass pull in welcome sunshine.*

ENSUITES

WALK-IN ROBES

LOOKING AFTER CLOTHES

You can spend a lot of time and money on what you wear, so it makes good sense to look after your investments. Following the care instructions on the clothing's label is the first step; washing colours and whites separately pays dividends, too. You should place delicate pieces in a lingerie bag before putting them through the machine on a gentle cycle, or simply hand-wash them.

Dryclean items when it's needed, rather than after every wear, as their colour and durability may be affected. And always clean the pieces of a suit together to keep the colour a perfect match.

How you store clothing is important. Avoid cramming them in drawers or doubling them up on hangers if possible – they need room to breathe. Large timber hangers are ideal for keeping jackets in shape but may cause delicate items to permanently lose theirs. Padded 'grandma' hangers are a much better choice for delicate garments.

Keep wardrobes and drawers clean. Regular vacuuming will suck up the dust, hair and lint on which insects can feed, and also remove any insect eggs. A quick wipe with disinfectant will help knock out mould spores.

Mothballs and chemicals like paradichlorobenzene deter silverfish, moths and other insects; however, a gentler way to ward off moths is with cedar blocks. The essential oils in cedar repel adult moths; when the scent fades, simply sandpaper the block to release another burst. Sachets of lavender and rosemary can also be used against moths. Reactivate them every few months with a few drops of their essential oils.

Mould can also ruin clothes. If your home suffers from damp, put a container of moisture-absorbing crystals in your wardrobe and also air the cupboard regularly.

Storing out-of-season clothes frees up space in your wardrobe and also protects winter woollies during summer, when insects are most active. Ensure clothes are washed before you pack them away in clean, dry, airtight containers or vacuum-sealed bags – even the smallest spot of dirt, food or ironing starch can attract insects and mildew. Add an insect repellent, mothballs or sachets of herbs or cedar shavings, and keep the boxes somewhere cool and well ventilated to prevent the clothes becoming musty.

Remember that leather should never be stored in a plastic bag. It encourages mildew and bacteria and will ruin the leather. Instead, keep leather items in a cool, dry place away from heat, and store leather garments in a breathable bag.

I Fitted out like a designer boutique, this dressing room makes choosing an outfit easy. A custom-made tie cabinet in American walnut not only gives an exclusive 'shop' feel but also keeps ties rolled and crease-free – the best way to store them. Twin cupboards for 'him' and 'her' ensure no fights for hanger space.

1 Exposed storage turns your favourite accessories into display pieces. This ingenious design carefully separates styles and colours while leaving your fashion collection on show. Private pieces and delicates can be stored behind select cupboard doors. The open hanging space allows clothing to breathe.

2 A mix of open and closed storage in a room is the most versatile. This dressing room features a geometric tie rack between cupboards and drawers. The ties' vibrant colours and patterns are displayed to full effect.

STORAGE

Ordered spaces allow

you to spend more time on important things and less time looking for your socks

THE ART OF STORAGE AND ORDER

An orderly home – with just enough clutter to be interesting – encourages you to relax. For some people 'order' means investing in built-in cabinets, for others it's simply labelling containers in the pantry. But by setting up a few easy storage systems, you can give your home a sense of space and prevent it from becoming an energy-sapping mess. It can even smooth out relationships as everyone has a place for their possessions and knows where to find things.

The simple act of living generates 'stuff'. Putting things in order is not about removing all the clutter, but rather giving it a home. Deciding where to begin is often the hardest part. Instead of launching into a crazed culling, use a more systematic approach.

Try making a list (just making the list will help you feel supremely organised). Define the problem areas in your home and jot down the items in each room, then decide what really needs to be where. Be realistic rather than ruthless. Banishing all sporting equipment to the garage may clear out the laundry, but make it inaccessible for the children. Pare things back to the essentials, then decide on a storage system.

You may like to draw the room to scale and play with different storage set-ups. Decide on how much open versus closed storage you want. For example, in the living room books add warmth and character, but unbroken rows of them can look oppressive. Breaking up long shelves with occasional uprights will create smaller boxes where you can display favourite pieces. In the kitchen, crockery is best kept in drawers or cupboards, as open shelving attracts dust and grease. Having an appliance cupboard where you keep the jug, toaster and food processor also frees up a lot of bench space.

Items that are used every day (like kitchen appliances) should be stored at waist height, with less-used items on higher shelves. Try storing things near where they're used – you're more likely to put them away. And remember, labels work particularly well with small items and make it easy to put them back in the correct spot.

Where you locate storage is an art in itself. Wall and ceiling spaces are often underused and racks, hooks and shelves can help you clear the floor. Built-in cabinets are great space-savers and can be finished with rich veneers so that they look more like furniture than utilitarian storage. Matching kitchen cupboards to those in the living area also gives a home a more cohesive feel. In smaller bathrooms, wall-hung cupboards keep the floor clear to make the room look larger.

While storage is an investment, it need not be expensive. A few lateral measures around the house, from linen cupboard to wardrobe, can make all the difference. In the bedroom, consider storing your bulky winter blankets and clothes in vacuum-sealed bags. They will take up a fraction of the space and be protected from dust and moths. And by replacing just a few pieces of furniture with more multipurpose units, such as a coffee table with drawers, both clutter and cost are reduced.

Granted, most homes can't be sparkling clean and tidy all the time, but adequate storage will help you manage the mess without the stress. With everything in its place, there's a good deal more time for rest and relaxation.

3

1 Storage is important for display as well as containing clutter. In this youngster's private space, pigeonhole shelving gives easy access to favourite toys and books, while clothing is kept behind closed doors. It's still a kid's room, but one that's very easy to keep tidy.

2 Bedtime essentials are clustered on this beautiful bedside table. A pile of books, reading lamp, scented candle, water carafe and cup make staying in this bed easy. Grouping items in odd numbers creates a balanced look for a display. Here, a square frame is hung low to connect it with the bedside collection.

3 Storage can be practical without looking utilitarian. In this little girl's bedroom, an old-fashioned travelling trunk is used as a wardrobe. It's a romantic element that can fire a little one's imagination with dreams of adventure in the 'olden days'.

Displaying favourite pieces, collected over the years, turns a house into a home by

1 An antique chest at the end of the bed is convenient storage for winter blankets, keeping them close by for when the weather turns cold. The quilts and piled cushions are also stowed in the timber trunk when the bed is undressed for sleeping.

2 Identical cupboards placed on each side of a fireplace give a sense of balance to this bedroom, and it is balance that makes you feel centred and at ease. A similarly measured effect could be achieved by offsetting a large storage unit with two smaller pieces.

3 Extending a decorative element to a storage piece is an easy way to incorporate it into a scheme. The wardrobe in this pretty pink room features panels of a fabric also used for the upholstered chair, blinds and bedcover. While strict themes are too rigid for some people, their repetition may inspire a calm sense of order.

encouraging fond memories

HERB PILLOW

YOU'LL NEED

- 25cm x 90cm-wide main fabric
- 15cm x 90cm-wide contrast fabric
- bias binding in 3 colours (braid, lace or rickrack is also suitable)
- 2 cups uncooked rice mixed with dried herbs for filling (good herbs to use are lemon verbena, lavender, cloves and rosemary)

METHOD

1. Cut the main fabric into two pieces, each 16cm x 23cm. Cut one piece of contrast fabric, 9cm x 14cm.

2. Position the contrast fabric in the middle of one of the pieces of main fabric, then sew in place.

3. Sew layers of bias binding, one at a time, around the middle panel. Sew the opposite sides first for neater corners. Alternatively, edge the middle panel with a single layer of bias binding, braid, lace or rickrack.

4. Place the pieces of main fabric right sides together, then stitch a seam 1.5cm in from the edge, leaving a small opening.

5. Fill the pillow with rice and herbs, then stitch the opening closed.

MAKE IT @ HOME

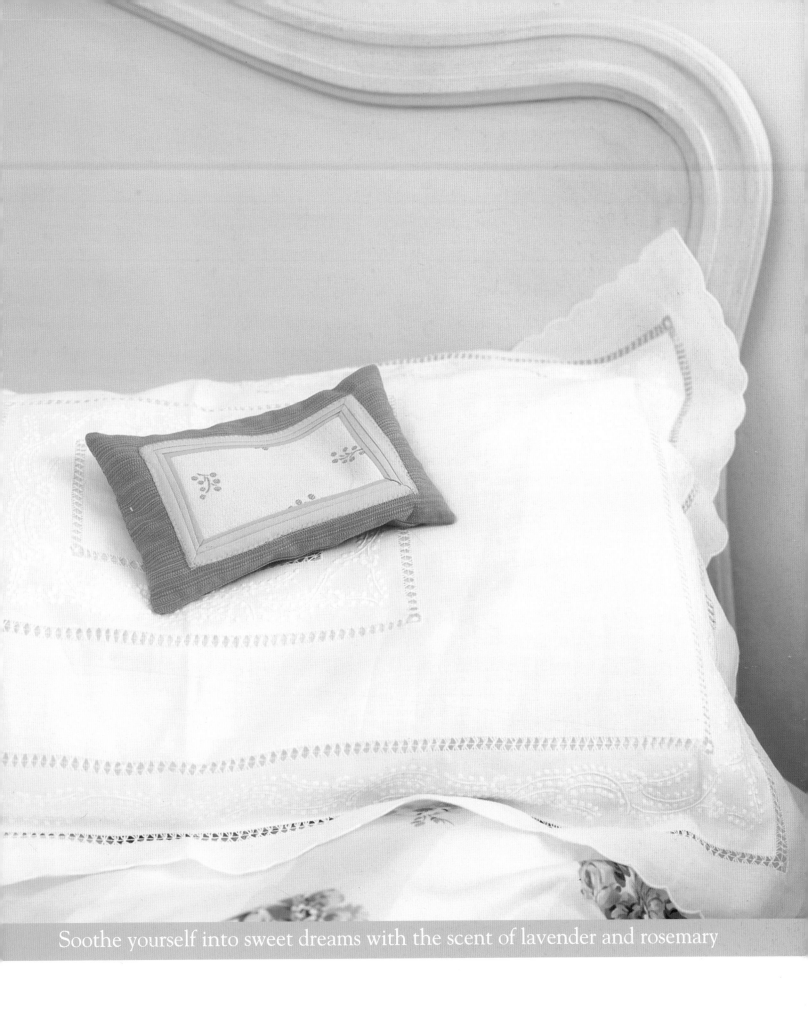

Soothe yourself into sweet dreams with the scent of lavender and rosemary

JEWELLERY ROLL

YOU'LL NEED

- 50cm x 90cm-wide main fabric for outside
- 50cm x 90cm-wide contrast fabric for inside (use soft, fine fabrics for best results)
- three 15cm nylon zips to match the inside fabric
- a press-stud
- beads to use as trims
- ribbon or piping to tie around the roll

METHOD

1 Cut one 40cm x 24cm piece from the main fabric for the outside of the roll. Cut one 40cm x 24cm piece from the contrast fabric for the inner lining.

2 Cut pieces for pockets from the contrast fabric. Cut one 4cm x 24cm, and three 15cm x 24cm. Cut ring-holder strip, 6cm x 20cm.

3 Pin together the pocket pieces to make one strip of fabric (see diagram below). Stitch seams 7cm in from each edge, leaving a 15cm gap in the middle of each to accommodate a zip. Sew in the zips.

4 Sew the inner lining to the back of the finished pocket piece, attaching the right side of the lining to the wrong side of the pocket piece.

5 Sew two lines of stitching across the inside piece, 1cm away from each zip, to separate the pockets and allow easy folding of the jewellery roll into thirds.

6 Sew ring-holder strip into a tube and turn right-side out. Stitch the raw end of the tube to one side of the inside piece, next to the middle zip. Sew on a press-stud to secure the free end of the ring-holder to the inside of the roll.

7 With right sides facing, sew the outside piece to the inside piece, leaving a 10cm gap on one side to allow turning out to right side. Trim corners and seams to a minimum, then turn the roll right-side out. Iron seams, then close the gap with hand-stitching.

8 Stitch around the outside of the jewellery roll, 1cm in from the edge.

9 Trim the zip tags and ring-holder with beads. Sew beads to the outside edge of the roll and sew a ribbon loop in place to secure the folded bag.

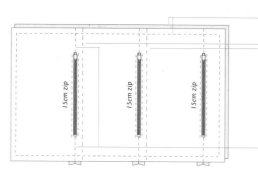

inner lining is attached to the back of the finished pocket piece

stitch across both pieces to seal pockets

15cm zip · 15cm zip · 15cm zip

7cm seams

MAKE IT @ HOME

Make a special holder for your favourite jewels to keep them safe and clean

REVIVE & RELISH

You can expend a lot of energy trying to be all things to all people. But you also need to look after yourself, to allocate space and time that is just for you. Only then can you truly be of help to those you love. ~ It's important to create places of pleasure and inspiration in your home, whether it's a reading room or study, a music den or special corner where you can display and admire a unique collection. If something makes you smile, then give it a place in your abode. ~ Embrace what you enjoy. Reconnect with yourself, your family and even your pets – all will make you happy. Be productive in your work, too; if you have a home office, make sure it's streamlined and well organised. ~ Having a special place of your own, no matter how small, is a joy that will help revive your spirit.

PERSONAL SPACES

1 *Daydreaming comes easily in a place like this. The classic Le Corbusier chaise is positioned to take in the magnificent ocean view and lull its occupant into a chilled-out frame of mind.*

2 *Wide open spaces, fresh air and vistas of lush green bush make the country a wonderful getaway. If you are lucky enough to have a holiday refuge or country home, get the most out of the personal time and space it affords. Make breakfast or morning tea an outdoor event and take time to soak up the view.*

previous page
Like their owners, pets love a private corner bathed in sunshine. While this Jack Russell terrier has claimed a beautiful French sofa, you may like to keep the furniture for yourself and instead designate a floor cushion in the sun for your favourite pooch.

As the world rages, find a place at home where you can be still

1 Colour brings vibrancy to an outdoor retreat. In this courtyard, colourful walls, a mosaic floor and beautiful blooms could not fail to dispel a jaded mood. The orange fence sets off the espaliered tangelos and showy dahlias. The vivid blue table and mosaic insets pump up the contrast. Think about seasonal changes when you create a colourful garden; these maple trees will turn a brilliant red in autumn.

2 A more secretive, closed-in area works well as a personal hideaway. This pergola includes a slatted panel which provides privacy but allows the little haven to remain open to the surrounds.

3 A beautiful corner is made all the more dreamy with floaty sheer curtains. Although only a whisper of fabric, sheers can be used to screen areas and afford privacy without blocking either sunlight or breezes.

4 Almost any outdoor space can be made your own, but a sheltered area with a little storage for tools or gardening equipment is more practical. This rustic collection of timber boxes and baskets is arranged on an old hall table. Remember a spot for the trusty gumboots, too.

A ROOM OF ONE'S OWN

In a perfect world, everyone would have their own 'decompression chamber' – a space where you could take time out, be free of stress and do something you really enjoy. It should be the ultimate sanctuary; whether it's a space in which you can be still and daydream, or a room where you can enjoy exercise, sewing or making music.

Your personal space doesn't need to be big to be nurturing – a quiet corner of a room that catches the sun and enjoys a pleasant view can be a haven. A window seat, a verandah, the kitchen (when it's not filled with family), a comfortable chair in the living area ... all can become chill-out zones.

Soothe your senses with touchable textures and calming colours. Use wool, sisal or jute underfoot rather than static-inducing synthetics, and keep a few cushions around to make things more comfortable when you're sitting in your favourite chair or lounging on the floor. Dress a wall with a length of beautiful fabric, or frame the material so that it works as a piece of art. Include something you love – a piece of art, furniture, a book or a photo. Finally, enjoy a favourite scent by bringing in an arrangement of flowers or herbs, or adding essential oils to an oil-burner.

Often it's the bedroom that's a sanctuary. The most important item in this room is obviously a good bed. But for a bedroom to cater for things other than sleeping, it needs a little more. Your downtime will be more pleasant if you include a comfortable chair and have adaptable lighting so you can dim the room for meditation or focus a stronger light for reading or other tasks. Keep the bedroom free of dust and air the mattress regularly so sensitive noses don't get agitated. And if you want to exercise in your bedroom, make sure you have adequate floor space and elbow room.

If you share the bedroom, you might want to find another nook of your own in the home. Choose a place where you can enjoy a few of your favourite things or indulge in a hobby. A garden shed or garage can be a place to reconnect with your interests. Make it comfortable, with adequate heating and cooling, so that you want to go there. These spaces are often shared with storage, so clear a space and add some favourite pieces, like a memento or a favourite photo, to differentiate your particular spot.

Unless you're an incurable clutterbug, your personal space will be more rewarding if you keep it ordered. Every time you see piles of paper and mess, you're reminded that they need attention – and that's not a relaxing thought! So include some storage in your personal space; a clear surface is wonderful for soothing the mind.

Remember that partners, housemates and children also need time and a space of their own. A play area, library or music 'room' can be easily integrated into a living area, a guest bedroom or some other underused space. That special place could be the perfect venue for items that are appreciated only by their owner, for example, his collection of sports memorabilia and her vintage quilts.

With a zone of your own (or one each!) you have a place to just be you. So feel relaxed, creative, and combine whatever makes you smile.

1 This spare bedroom, with its tranquil view of treetops, has become a personal meditation room. Meditation is easier in a place that's free of distractions, so aim for a simple scheme. It helps to be neither too hot nor too cold. Here, central heating is used to maintain a pleasant temperature. Incense or aromatherapy oils can be used to enhance your contemplation.

2 Making a space your own can be as simple as having your own armchair. In this living room, period pieces are set against a neutral scheme, with the Louis-style chair given a prime position in front of the fireplace.

3 Simple but effective, this garden room is a great place to rest between plantings. A soothing space needn't be elaborately decorated: here a single chair and woollen blanket are both snug and practical. A trolley contains all that's needed for potting up plants, and its height is good for avoiding back strain.

4 Open the door on your personal retreat and let natural light weave its magic. French doors make a moody play of light and shadow in this charming room. Opening windows and doors also encourages natural ventilation and brings freshness to the indoors.

Sanctuary means not only creating a calming space but also finding the time to use it

1 *Located between two bedrooms, this deck area offers outdoor relaxation for the whole household. The soft sound of water trickling down the stone feature wall and into a fishpond brings another soothing element to the mix. Cushions can be fetched from the bedrooms to make things more comfortable.*

2 *A side passage becomes a quiet retreat with the addition of folding teak chairs. This tree-planted area is quite small, but a mirror positioned on the wall behind the chairs gives an illusion of space and reflects light into the dining room.*

SUNROOMS

1 Removing all the barriers between indoor and outdoor living spaces maximises a brilliant view. Glass stretches to the eaves, opening the house to the sky, while a teak deck extends seaward. Bi-fold doors may be opened to reveal all.

2 A glazed wall makes an outdoor pond seem part of this living area. The pool's cool purples and greys are repeated indoors, strengthening the connection between the two spaces. Having a view to a water feature brings some of its serenity inside.

Make daydreaming in the sun one of your favourite pastimes

MUSIC AT HOME

Music is an energy ever-present in our lives and it has some remarkable qualities. It can lower your blood pressure, calm unruly children, promote healing, reduce stress, help concentration and even – some studies claim – increase your intelligence. While styles of music may change (just last century there was jazz, blues, swing, folk, rock'n'roll, hip-hop and rap), music itself is always a powerful force.

"Rhythm and harmony find their way to the inmost soul," wrote Plato, and while no-one's quite sure how or why it has this effect, music is capable of triggering intense emotions and responses. When listening to music, your brain becomes highly active on both sides, unlike many other activities which stimulate the right or left side of the brain only. Scientists have also discovered an organ in the human ear called a sacculus, which triggers hunger and hedonistic responses in the brain. You don't use this organ for hearing, but it does respond to certain frequencies in music, which might explain why certain styles of music are so arousing.

Music's emotive effect has always been recognised, but the way you actually listen to music in your home is changing with technology. CDs, which replaced vinyl records in the 1980s, are now being superseded by SACDs (Superior Audio CDs) that better emulate the warm, rich tone of the analogue recordings previously heard on vinyl. MP3s, which store music in a digital file format, mean music can now be downloaded off the internet and onto your computer or a portable MP3 player, although most of these MP3s don't yet match the sound quality of a CD recording. Music DVDs allow you to watch video clips and read biographies on the television screen while you listen to the surround-sound, which supposedly re-creates the effect of a concert hall.

The hard drive on your computer can store up to 900 hours of recorded music in digital form (closer to 3000 hours in a compressed format), so your entire music collection can be downloaded and stored for on-call access. A hard drive in your study could be linked with speakers throughout the house, letting you enjoy hours of mellow jazz or upbeat tunes without having to change a CD.

A centralised audio-visual system, with speakers installed throughout the home, lets you blend music with your lifestyle. Keypads in each room control the individual output in each room. What's more, you can integrate lights, security and other electronically controlled devices into the same system.

Listening to music may be therapeutic, but playing an instrument can be almost cathartic. Making music is a passionate pastime, whether it's on a piano, guitar or drums. Your sanctuary should afford you the privacy to experiment, practise and express yourself through music. You may not have the luxury of a dedicated music room, so instead borrow some time in an area away from the distractions of the living area, such as a home office or guest bedroom. A piano, however, may still need to take pride of place in the living area. If this is the case, try to allocate 'personal' and 'public' time for this room to avoid any conflicts.

Music creates a special ambience in the home and brings a great deal of pleasure, whether you're tickling the ivories or sinking into a bath to the sounds of Mozart. As William Shakespeare wrote, 'If music be the food of love, play on.'

3

1 A sunroom can be the perfect place to revive and make music. Fresh air stimulates the mind, daylight enhances concentration and the leafy view offers natural inspiration. The soft golden hue in this room has an ethereal feel that's in harmony with strumming a harp.

2 A baby grand piano is placed in this sunlit entrance foyer, giving a splendid first impression to visitors. In an open-plan home, half-walls or partitions may be used to grant private nooks and personal space for passions and hobbies. This music 'room' is partitioned off the living area to grant seclusion while encouraging a flow of beautiful music.

3 Make listening to music a favourite pastime, with an inviting chaise longue and a room with a view. In this sunroom, a large wall-window frames the bushland outlook. A feature wall painted a deep rum colour and floors in Tasmanian oak keep the interior cosy, whatever the season.

READING ROOMS

1 Antique books, with their elaborate embossed covers and mysterious past, add charm to any library. Even in ancient times, repositories of clay tablets were kept in domestic houses. It seems that home has always been the best place to read and revive.

2 A regal mix of burgundy and gold creates an exclusive 'club' feel in this home library. The colours are well suited to the mix of antique furniture, portraits and collections of china. Books line the walls and frame the window, adding a scholarly feel but not overwhelming the space.

3 This contemporary reading room occupies a mezzanine level. It's a secluded space bathed in sunshine, and with a pair of comfortable '60s-style armchairs, it's irresistible to any bookworm.

4 Books can be used for more than just a great read. In this corner, a collection of old books is used as part of a display on an art deco hall table. Second-hand volumes create a homely, intimate feel. When using books decoratively, base the collection on a tonal mix.

1 *Tucked into a sunny corner, this home office is streamlined to maximise space. A laptop removes the need for a bulky desktop computer and accessories, and is easily stored. Music is incorporated into the scheme by mounting units and speakers on the wall. A compact design like this is particularly good when your work space is part of a living area.*

2 *When decorating your home office, surround yourself with things you love. By using objects or furnishings that make you happy, you're more inclined to want to be in that space – and hopefully do some work. Having artworks and other pieces to look at in your office also stops you staring at the computer screen all day. A model ship is well suited to the style of this traditional study.*

1

2

HOME WORK

Let your home office have a view, sunshine and great-looking furniture

WORKING FROM HOME

Working from home has become an accepted part of life. According to the Australian Bureau of Statistics, in 2000, one in five workers (1.8 million people) worked some hours at home, and one million people did most of their work from home.

You'll increase your gross domestic happiness by making your home office a place you want to be. Instead of shoving your computer in a dark corner with down-at-heel office cast-offs, let your SOHO (small office home office) have a view, fresh air, sunshine and great-looking furniture. If possible, locate it away from the everyday hurly-burly of the house. If you have clients visiting, it's best if your office has a separate entrance, or at least a direct route from the front door. Don't have an office space in your bedroom, as you need to maintain a division between work and rest.

Colour has a big effect on mood so use it to your advantage. Yellow brings a sense of energy, while softer oranges and reds make a space warm and comfortable. Blues, lavenders and neutral tones promote a sense of calm and balance.

Aromatherapy oils can also get you in the mood for work. Peppermint, lemon, eucalyptus and cinnamon are said to stimulate concentration and improve memory. Lavender and bergamot help ease tension, while basil promotes mental stamina.

Try to have a large 'uncramped' desk in your work area – small spaces can lead to clutter and disorganisation. Keep paperwork in check with priority trays and put a cork board on the inside of a cupboard to replace walls of post-it notes. Allocate enough storage for files and books, too, even if it's in an area away from your computer.

Be nice to your body. Take a short break every hour and invest in an ergonomic chair to give your back, neck and shoulders proper support. When you sit at a computer, your thighs should be horizontal (shorter people should have a footrest), your elbows should be bent at 90 degrees, and you should be looking straight ahead at the middle of the screen. Position your computer side-on to any windows to avoid hotspots on your screen or looking into the sun, and have a good level of general light in the room.

Working at home can be rewarding, but it's easy to get distracted. To counter this, set yourself a routine. Taking a walk around the block in the morning lets you make the psychological transition from home to work before you start the day. Disciplining yourself to work between certain times and do domestic chores at other times, say, after 5pm, increases productivity, too. Finally, don't cram in your life around work; instead put exercise and social time in your diary and arrange your work around these.

Increase your productivity by making your home office a place you want to be

1 'Her' work space is a bright, functional corner of the living space. A view of the garden stimulates thought, while further inspiration is close at hand thanks to an abundance of storage for books. The cube-inspired cabinet has a mix of concealed and displayed storage – ideal for shared living and working areas.

2 This home office is tucked under the ceiling, just a flight of stairs above the living area. Keeping your SOHO a little separate from the busyness of family life allows you the quiet needed to concentrate on work. Fresh air and sunlight are also essential; here, they are provided by an opening skylight.

3 This work space is designed for instant correspondence, with a computer replacing the pen and paper, and email the stamp. Little storage is needed, allowing more room for decorative touches.

4 Projecting a professional image to clients is an important factor when you're working from home. This contemporary office incorporates a meeting area that's sophisticated yet comfortable. If your office tends to be in a constant state of chaos, use a separate space such as a dining room for meetings.

4

TAKING TIME OUT

The modern woman's cry of being 'all things to all people', and putting in time at work while also carrying the load at home, can lead to weary body, mind and spirit. So clear the diary for a special date with a very important person – you. Me-time will help you tap into your dreams and feelings, or simply let you chill out and recharge.

Set a special scene for your personal time – the more indulgent, the better. Fill the room with music you love and beautiful scents to lift your spirits. Be yourself in this space; feel free to sing, dance and have some fun on your own. For a more pampering experience, treat yourself to a long hot bubble bath, pedicure or facial.

Try keeping a journal by your bed to record your thoughts or feelings. Self-expression can also come through painting, drawing, cooking, sewing or taking to the toolkit. Or go for a long walk to give yourself time alone with your thoughts.

Whatever takes your fancy, from a quiet coffee alone to a weekly gardening session, make the time to reconnect with yourself.

1 *De-cluttering your work area can restore a sense of control and increase your concentration. With messy piles of paper kept in check – in this office they are stored in groovy stainless-steel drawers – you can introduce things to inspire and keep you motivated, such as an artwork over the desk or magazines that spark ideas.*

2 *Some work spaces are more appropriate for occasional use than the hustle and bustle of everyday business. Here, rows of books are made interesting by colour placement – not altogether practical for a working office but visually stimulating nonetheless. As a 'thinking' zone, this corner excels with its striking tangerine chair, quirky collectables and display of vibrant artworks.*

3 *The niche made by this window arch provides a perfect nook for a home office. Built-in storage maximises the usefulness of this tiny space, holding the computer, files, books and other office equipment. An upholstered dining chair and organza curtains give a decorative twist that matches the living room, while still being fabulously functional.*

3

Put social time in your diary and arrange your work time around it

A garden shed could be a garden room, workshop, hobby room or studio space –

1 *A carpet of lavender extends from this cottage and fills the air with fragrance. A craft shed in the garden can be used to launch a home-business. Be creative with what your patch of earth can yield, considering such options as supplying fresh blooms, drying or pressing flowers or distilling oils.*

2 *The simple garden shed is not so simple any more. This aluminium shed is a modern take on the cottage style. Its cool grey is in subtle contrast to the colours of the thriving garden. Timber gives a more natural look to a garden shed, while bright hues could be chosen to pick up the colours of your favourite blooms.*

make it your own GARDEN SHEDS

HAPPINESS WITH PETS

As social creatures, humans derive much happiness from time spent with loved ones – including the furry, winged or gilled variety. Pets provide companionship, love and loyalty – and mostly without criticism. For many people, a pet is part of the family.

Sharing your time and affection with a pet makes you feel good, and research suggests it also improves your health. Studies by the Baker Medical Research Institute in Melbourne found that pet owners had lower blood pressure and cholesterol than people without pets. Just patting a dog or cat can lower blood pressure.

Pets are a responsibility, too. They depend on you for love, food and shelter, and you want them to be content. Do some research to find a pet and breed that will be happy with your living arrangements and lifestyle. If you decide on a specific breed, get in touch with a breeder to get some more information before you make a final decision. Although each animal is an individual, certain breeds of dogs and cats are more suited to living indoors or outdoors, or prefer living with a couple to a noisy family home.

Remember, too, that dog- or cat-protection societies and sometimes vets have adult animals that need homes. Taking on a loving grown-up pet can be just as satisfying, and far less messy, than training a kitten or puppy.

Whatever pets you live with, spend time playing or talking with them, and take your dog on walks regularly. Happiness is reciprocal; by making a pet feel special and loved you will be rewarded with a happy, faithful friend.

1 *Animals can play a vital role in making your home more of a sanctuary. They encourage you to take time out and spice things up with their own personalities. This hen-house is home to a pet rooster and keeps him safe from the cheeky cattle dog. It also provides a safe place for hens to lay their eggs.*

2 *A gazebo is the garden shed's posh cousin, with it main purpose being for relaxation rather than pottering. This gazebo follows a traditional design, although its poolside position is less conventional, as these little huts were first used in gardens. Yet it's still a great place to retreat from the wind (or just get away from the pool crowd) and enjoy the sunshine.*

Getting out in the garden is a way to reconnect with yourself and nature

POTTING HERBS

YOU'LL NEED

- small ceramic pots
- herb seedlings (such as thyme, basil, sage, oregano and lavender)
- potting mix
- slow-release fertiliser granules
- water-saving crystals
- watering-can
- label stakes (available from the garden section of large stores and nurseries)

METHOD

1 Fill each pot with potting mix. Add some slow-release fertiliser granules to keep the plants well nourished, plus some water-retaining crystals to help retain moisture – these are especially useful if the pots are sitting on a windowsill in direct sunlight.

2 Plant the seedlings halfway down into the pots. Remember that once oregano and thyme grow, they will cascade over the edge of the pot.

3 Water in the plants, using 1 litre of water for each pot. Stake in a label for each herb. Check the soil every day and keep it moist with regular watering. You may like to place the pot on a saucer filled with pebbles to stop the water leaking everywhere. The pebbles raise the pot above the water and prevent the herbs getting 'soggy feet'.

TIP *Herbs need to be harvested frequently, so place them at eye level, or somewhere where you are guaranteed to see them. That way you can pick the leaves with ease and you'll remember to water them regularly.*

MAKE IT @ HOME

THYME

Growing your own herbs is immensely satisfying. Start with a few pots and progress...

SCRAPBOOKING

YOU'LL NEED

- scrapbook
- scissors
- craft glue
- assorted buttons
- lettering
- coloured paper
- stencils
- anything else that takes your fancy in a craft store

METHOD

1   Deciding on the contents of your scrapbook is the hardest part. Thinking of subjects will help as you make your decision. These can include weddings, elementary years, pets, holidays, grandchildren and baby's first steps.

2   Choose a scrapbook. A journal, photo albums with removable pages or paper punched and tied together can all become a special memory book.

3   Decide on your theme and keep this in mind when shopping and sourcing ideas for materials. If you are making a scrapbook about your son, for example, look for stickers that identify with his hobbies, or papers that are in his favourite colours. Find your favourite picture of him and using lettering and layers, build a scrapbook of how you see the one you love. Remember that this is a book of your memories, so whatever you choose you will surely cherish the outcome.

4   Add comments and remarks as you assemble your book. This personalises it and adds to your memories. A nice idea is to leave an empty page with a pen tied on a ribbon, so people can add their own comments.

6   Display your masterpiece in your home, so that everyone can pick it up and flick through the memories.

MAKE IT @ HOME

A scrapbook is literally a memory book. Fill its pages with the story of your family

ENERGISE & EXCITE

Conversing with friends, listening to music or taking in an evocative artwork; enjoying the sweet touch of a cooling breeze floating down a hallway or the bright colours of flowers thrown casually into a tall vase. The very act of 'living' in your home can be cause for appreciation. ~ Be enthusiastic about all the possibilities contained within your own four walls. Make home a place that stimulates your mind as well as feeding your senses. ~ Inviting people you care about to share in your space will make it an even more vibrant and positive place to be. Treat them with generosity and respect and they'll be certain to return. Family, friends and nature all combine to bring energy to your home and your life.

1 A lot of a family's time can be spent on the sofa, so ensure it's as comfortable as can be. This suede sofa is dressed with soft, plump cushions and is positioned so that people face each other, rather than the television. It also has plenty of room for someone to stretch out with a good book.

2 Strong architectural lines provide a modern framework for this family room. The sun-filled, open-plan design encourages a flow of fresh air as well as conversation. Furnishings are kept simple to focus attention on the artworks; the pared-back scheme also accentuates the feeling of space in the room.

previous page
Asian fusion is a distinct style that combines the best of Australian and Asian looks. Here it's used to create a great space for both food and conversation. Timber bases under the two floor cushions are slid under the coffee table when not in use, while the cushions could be used on the chairs.

around to share good food and conversation is one of life's most rewarding activities

ENJOYING FAMILY LIFE

Home should be a haven. When life in the world outside is full of stress and difficult decisions, you want to be able to come home and just be yourself. For both adults and children, it's the place in the world where you hope to find unconditional love and a sense of security – home should be a place you can depend on.

That's the plan, anyway. If you've experienced that kind of home life yourself, you know how vital it is to your sense of wellbeing, and you'll want to create a similar environment for your own kids to help set them up for life.

One of the things that makes you feel secure is family dinners, where you can all sit together and chat about the day and what's on your mind. You might not be able to do that every night of the week, but try to do it as often as you can. For those evenings when it's not possible, don't leave the children to eat dinner on their own – be close by, doing whatever you have to do, and keep on chatting.

Psychologists have found that adults who have difficulty communicating often say they had no family discussions around the dinner table; it's a skill they haven't learnt.

And as for what you should be eating, let the kids have a say in it every now and then. If you simply ask them what they'd like for dinner, they'll probably want some sort of junk food, but tell them it's for a family dinner and it's more likely they'll request a roast. They really do know the difference.

To help create that warm family environment, turn off the television and put on some music. Think about it – aren't there pieces of music you hear now that take you straight back to your childhood? It's a brilliant way of building memories. Using television as a babysitter isn't a great idea, but watching the television as a family activity can be. Kids like nothing better than everyone watching together.

Pets can make a house feel like a home, too – and it's especially good if the children take some responsibility for them. It's an enjoyable way for kids to learn about caring for and respecting other creatures.

Respecting each other's privacy is also important. Everyone needs a place of their own to escape to sometimes, even children. So knock before entering someone else's bedroom, and don't feel it's your right to go through your kids' things or read their diaries. Of course, there may be something wrong if a child spends all their time in their room, so try to keep the lines of communication open.

Parents make most of the rules at home and have the final say. But involving the children as much as is practical in family decisions and the running of the house means that they'll feel it really is their home, which is just the way it should be.

1 Family-friendly doesn't mean unfashionable. Soft textures and an absence of sharp corners make this living area a safe one for kids (although that bowl of lollies could cause a bit of wildness). It's a room in which to be at ease. The beautiful roses and groovy furniture appeal to adults, while the children adore having a soft rug to roll on.

2 Light sweeps through this spacious home. To keep a cool flow of air in a lofty space such as this, set a skylight, ceiling vent or windows up high. Warm air can escape and cool air will be pulled in from outside to replace it. Without good ventilation, the air in upper levels can get stuffy and hot. Remember, sunlight energises and fresh air invigorates.

3 A family room should be a place for the imagination to thrive. This lively space combines a bounty of shapes, patterns and vivid colours to provoke conversation. While there are plenty of breakables, small children are still welcome here – it's a space for living, after all.

4 White is not forbidden in the family room, but choose washable paint and put stain protection on fabrics. White reflects light and gives a feeling of space. It's also a good base for people who enjoy changing the look of a room by swapping different accessories and soft furnishings.

5 Plush carpet gives a family space a touch of luxury. Here, the carpet acts as a colour feature: it tones in with the walls and provides a contrast to the light-coloured furniture and white feature wall. Carpet is an investment, so go for a quality option like wool; it is more durable and feels wonderful to touch.

1 This breezy home uses white and a natural palette to create a mood removed from the hassles of everyday life. The double-height room gives a sense of impressive space. An open breezeway, skylights and clerestory windows maintain a peaceful flow of light and air.

2 Cool tiles are perfect as flooring for formal living areas in warmer climates. In winter, rugs can be laid down. The sofas and tiles in this room share the same tone, making a quite compact area seem larger. Interest is added with patterned throws, which may be changed to suit the season. Arrangements of flowers and foliage bring a hint of the tropics indoors.

3 It's the mix of textures rather than colour which brings this formal living area alive. A glossy wall, finished in two-pack polyurethane, makes a wonderful contrast to the deeply tufted rug and the white leather on the sectional sofa and dining chairs. A painting over the sofa ties the room's colour and textures together, giving the space a dramatic focal point.

4 Beautiful architectural detailing has been painted white in this airy formal living area. The elegant decor is reminiscent of the romantic era of receiving rooms, salons and formal drawing rooms. A slightly darker tone of white helps define boundaries, such as the arch in this room.

FORMAL LIVING
Formal living areas hark back

4

to an era of receiving rooms and salons, and nowadays provide a sense of occasion

EMOTIONAL EFFECTS OF COLOUR

Feeling blue, pretty in pink, red with rage or green with envy? Chances are that colour has affected your mood or at least one decision you have made today, whether it was stopping at traffic lights or starting to feel hungry after you passed by a red-painted restaurant. Colour can have a powerful influence on the way you feel, evoking feelings of relaxation or stress, depending on the hue.

Colour is the visual spectrum of light, and the wavelengths in light are constantly vibrating. Since every colour vibrates at a different frequency, it makes sense that each affects you in a unique way. Take red, for example. Traditionally considered a passionate colour, red has the slowest vibration and largest waves, and people react strongly to it. That means red is fine if you want to be stimulated, but a bit overwhelming when you don't. Cool colours, such as blue and green, generally reduce body vibrations, so surround yourself with them when you want to feel calm.

Understanding your response to colour will greatly influence how you decorate your home. When you have a clear idea of the purpose of each room, and how active or relaxed you want to feel there, it's easier to choose an appropriate colour.

RED Passionate and intense, red boosts low energy levels, speeds pulse rates and stimulates the appetite. Use it with caution though, as red may overstimulate and cause irritation. It can be very energising when used in a large space but claustrophobic in a small room. You can 'heat up' a cold room by painting a feature wall red.

BLUE Relaxing and peaceful, blue slows the heartbeat and lowers blood pressure. It gives the impression of space and also soothes anxiety or stress. Use lighter shades of blue in your bedroom to encourage a good night's sleep. Avoid it if you're feeling low – blue can slow you down and make you feel melancholy (hence 'the blues').

PURPLE A royal colour of spirituality and mystery, purple is traditionally associated with highly evolved spirits. It's said to encourage intuition and dreaminess, which can be good in a study. Like blue, purple is wonderful for de-stressing, but it has a sensual element as well. Avoid using purple in rooms where lots of activity takes place.

YELLOW This colour increases your energy levels and creates a feeling of happiness. It encourages activity and quick thinking, so it's perfect for an office. It's one of the first colours a newborn baby can distinguish (after black and white tones) but is better used in their play area than in the bedroom. As with all warm hues, balance yellow with a cooler colour to discourage excessive stimulation.

ORANGE Gentler than red or yellow, orange is still stimulating and warm. It spans a huge range, from day-glo bright to rustic terracotta. Orange is said to aid digestion and rouse the appetite, so it's ideal for kitchens and dining rooms, especially in table settings and flowers. A sociable, fun-loving hue, orange makes an excellent antidepressant.

GREEN Green is a calming colour that's associated with the harmony found in nature. Its restful effect makes green ideal to use in rooms where you go to unwind or sleep. It is also seen as impartial, so it's an excellent choice for rooms where decision-making or discussions take place. However, too much green may inspire indifference or inertia, so you should use it sparingly or balance its effect with white.

1 Be creative with what you put in your main entertaining space. A brightly coloured ottoman, trinkets collected on your travels or bold paintings are fascinating points of interest and give everyone something to talk about.

2 Art demands light and space to be fully appreciated and this modern home, with its vibrant collection of original theatre posters, uses both to full effect. A few pieces of furniture pick up the bold colours in the prints without competing for attention or space.

After the corporate grey of the business world, stepping into a home that is full

2

of colour lifts your spirits

TRANSITION ZONES

1 *Apartment living means making the most of all spaces. This deep balcony, accessed through sliding doors, is furnished as an outdoor dining room. A few plants could also make it the garden, or a daybed could turn it into the perfect place for an afternoon siesta.*

2 *A modern light fitting makes a dramatic focal point in this lofty space. This living area has a lot of movement through it – it's on the route to the adjacent terrace and also to the front door. The constant foot traffic creates distractions, but the extravagant light shade gives this area its own particular character.*

VENTILATION AND BREEZEWAYS

A gentle breeze through the home does much more than cool you on a hot afternoon. Good airflow and ventilation brings in oxygen, removes odours and discourages disease. Just like you, a house needs a breath of fresh air to be healthy. Without good circulation, the air inside a home will become more humid, encouraging the growth of mould and the spread of germs.

Opening a window can freshen up one room, but unless you've designed a circuit for the airflow, that's all it will do. You could encourage the movement of air with cross-ventilation and by placing vents and windows close to the ceiling (clerestory windows or high louvres are ideal). The hot air rises and is pushed out of the house by the cooler air drawn in to replace it. In double-storey homes, an open staircase can help direct the airflow. Vents placed at each end of the roof cavity also encourage a flow of air that reduces the temperature under the roof and in the living areas below.

For good cross-ventilation, try opening windows and doors at opposite ends of a house to create a breezeway. Having open windows directly across from each other causes a draught, so instead direct the airflow through open doors to the rest of the house.

These natural alternatives are in keeping with the ideal of being in harmony with your surrounds. The German theory of *baubiologie* (building biology) takes it further by comparing the home to a living being that has skin and needs to breathe. The movement was pioneered by Professor Anton Schneider, who in 1976 set up his Institute for Building Biology and Ecology. It promotes natural building materials such as timber, clay and brick that are porous and allow for ventilation. Synthetic building materials, however, may contain harmful toxins. If your home is not made of 'breathing' materials, having some indoor plants can help to purify the air.

Architects often incorporate breezeways to promote a good natural airflow. In days gone by, breezeways were pergola-like areas with a fixed awning. Now, Zen-inspired atriums or interior courtyards create a thoroughfare for breezes. Wind cycles will also affect the design of a home. Rooms that face summer breezes should feature lots of windows while rooms open to winter winds should be protected by walls or trees.

Open-plan designs, where living areas open to the outdoors, also improve ventilation. Living areas should be oriented so they guide drier air from outside through to kitchens and bathrooms, the source of moisture and heat in homes. But don't just rely on a good breeze – you'll need an extractor fan, too, to dispel all the moist air from a bathroom or cooking odours from a kitchen. And while natural is best, extra cooling devices such as fans or airconditioners may still be needed in hot, humid climates.

Fresh air energises the mind and body, and good ventilation helps create a home conducive to health and happiness. Simply by opening a few windows you can clear your head, cut down on energy use and play your part in saving the environment.

Just like you, a house needs a breath of fresh air to be healthy

3

1 This upstairs living zone has a simple, unfussy scheme so that it makes an easy transition to the adjacent deck and bedrooms. It escapes the noise of a main living area and is a place to kick back and gather your thoughts or have a private conversation.

2 A courtyard is an urban alternative to a back garden. This outdoor space is made into a calm retreat with timber decking, rattan chairs and a splash of green. Houses that are laid out around a courtyard enjoy immense natural light and a lovely view. It's a wonderful start for creating a sanctuary.

3 Chic outdoor furniture makes seamless the transition between indoor and outdoor areas. The cool minimalist style is carried over with modish dining chairs and a sleek table. Water features and planters also repeat the interior's style and colours.

Getting together for a meal is the warmest way to cement relationships

1 *Formal with a twist of fun, this dining room provides plenty to marvel at, from the hoop-pine curved ceiling to the zinc-clad fireplace and built-in benches around the wall. When backgrounds are striking and furniture heavy, it's best to keep tables unadorned. This red-gum table is left bare deliberately, adding another contrast to the timber mix.*

2 *Warehouse living has a certain energy about it, but the open-plan layout requires some thought when it comes to furnishings. It's essential that the dining area harmonises with the living area to give a home coherence. In this warehouse conversion, the vibrant blue used in the living area is toned down for the dining space, with a softer hue used for a calmer effect.*

DINING ROOMS

I *Dining in this open-plan kitchen-living zone can be dressed up or down. The dining setting seats eight easily, and the cook can still converse with the guests while preparing the food. Bright red kitchen stools tucked under the breakfast bar provide a perch for casual get-togethers or extra seating when entertaining.*

ETIQUETTE FOR TODAY

Rules of etiquette have relaxed in recent years but that's no reason to ignore good manners. Etiquette is more about making other people feel special and appreciated than knowing which glass to use with what wine. When you're talking to someone, either at work or when you're socialising, always be attentive and always make eye contact. If you're moving on at a function, say 'excuse me' and make sure someone else has taken your place. When attending a party you should try to take a gift for your hosts, such as a good bottle of wine or flowers. Always RSVP to an invitation, either in writing or with a phone call, and afterwards send a note or email of thanks.

Mobile phones are the latest etiquette offenders. They should be switched off when you're in the cinema and at the very least muted when you're out to dinner, in a lift or on public transport. And remember, a loud mobile phone conversation is as obnoxious as breathing in someone else's cigarette smoke.

Extend good manners to your neighbours, too. Present a clean house and yard and observe rubbish disposal and noise guidelines. Let them know about any potentially noisy activities, like a party or renovations, to maintain neighbourhood harmony. The heart of etiquette, after all, is consideration of others.

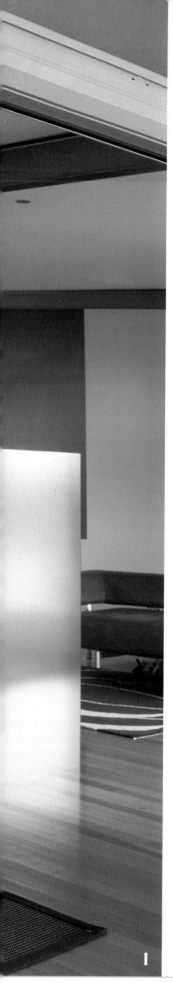

1 *Square tables are becoming increasingly popular. Like round tables they don't have someone sitting at the 'head' and they promote an easy interaction between the diners. This eight-seater has timber the same colour as the kitchen cupboards, giving the space a visual unity.*

2 *Waterfront dining is a restaurant drawcard and it's most inviting in your own home, too. This sunny dining room overlooks a tranquil pool and courtyard. Concertina doors open to give an alfresco feel in warm weather, but the water views may be enjoyed year round.*

Preparing and sharing food is a beautiful way of showing your appreciation of others

1 *Colour is a great tool for uniting spaces. This living room and adjacent dining area make pretty partners in lilac and baby pink. Fresh flowers on the formal dining table are a perfect match with the sofa cushions, and napery could also be tied into the theme. Four groovy cubes are stored under the coffee table for more casual dinner dates.*

2 *Big is beautiful when it comes to the dining table; this one seats at least 12 people. With so many personalities around one table, you should make the space equally lively. This room has fresh flowers to lift the spirits and yellow to give a warm, welcoming feel. Proportion is important when dealing with big numbers and here a large painting balances the scheme.*

FLOWERS AND PLANTS IN THE HOME

Fresh flowers and plants make your home a living, breathing sanctuary. Indoor plants like *Spathiphyllum* lilies, gerberas and many of the *Dracaena* family are particularly good at absorbing toxic vapours from the air inside buildings. These chemicals are released from varnishes, paints, floorcoverings, plywoods and many other everyday objects ... even tissues and paper towels. Plants also add moisture and oxygen to the atmosphere, creating a healthier living environment for you and your family.

The colour and fragrance of cut flowers make you feel good on a more emotional level. For example, the citrus scent of mimosa is uplifting, while a rose's fragrance is rich, soft and soothing. Generally, pale flowers have strong scents as they use perfume, rather than colour, to attract insects – just think of gardenias and jasmine.

An arrangement of flowers or leaves also look wonderful. Their colours and perfect forms bring delight to any interior. Buying some flowers for yourself is well worth the money for the pleasure it brings. Even when it's taken inside, nature sure is grand.

Decorating with fresh flowers brings colour and scent into a home

ARRANGING FLOWERS

YOU'LL NEED

- pink and white lisianthus (*Eustoma grandiflorum*) with 3-4 florets open in the bunch
- flower preserver or flower food
- vase
- gardening shears or a sharp knife

METHOD

1   Remove packaging. Cut away any foliage on the stems below the waterline and remove any damaged foliage or flowers.

2   Cutting diagonally with a sharp knife, not scissors, cut 2.5 to 5cm from the end of each stem.

3   Three-quarters fill a vase with tepid water and add the flower food.

4   Arrange flowers in a rounded, spilling form. Place those with a curved stem around the rim of the vase. If the flowers are all the same height, cut eight of the stems shorter so that there is some variation.

MAKE IT @ HOME

Even a simple posy can remind you of springtime and bring on a smile

EMBELLISHING NAPKINS

YOU'LL NEED

To make four napkins:

- 1 metre x 90cm-wide washable fabric
- embroidery cottons and ribbon
- 1 metre ribbon for tie

METHOD

1 Cut fabric for each napkin 42cm x 42cm.

2 Turn a 1cm hem all around and machine-stitch in place. For neater corners, sew opposite sides of the napkin first. To avoid bulky corners, cut a small triangle from each corner before turning the remaining hems.

3 Following the photograph, embroider a small flower motif on one corner of each napkin, using embroidery cottons, embroidery ribbons or beads.

4 Fold the napkin, tie with a ribbon, and add a fresh flower if you like.

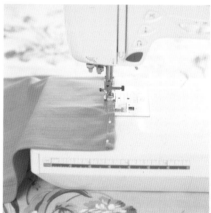

MAKE IT @ HOME

Place settings are made warm and welcoming with flower-stitched napkins

ENJOY & ENTERTAIN

Your home is a place for sharing the very best things – laughter, food, stories and time. While it's easy to be caught up in a daily whirl of obligations, try to remember what it's really about. Friends and family are your anchors in life, so keep those bonds strong. ~ Stay in touch by inviting people over for a meal, a coffee or just to watch a movie. Throw open your home whenever you can. Plump the cushions, add some fresh blooms and fill the house with wonderful scents to welcome your guests. ~ Modern entertaining is casual and relaxed, with lazy lunches and no-fuss dinners the order of the day. You could congregate in the kitchen or use your garden as an outdoor dining room. However you choose to do it, enjoy your home with your loved ones as you entertain.

Much of today's home life is spent in the kitchen, so make it a light-filled centre

1 *Two island benches prove better than one in this capacious kitchen. The wide central bench is a useful work space while the high breakfast bar has its own dishwasher, sink and appliance cupboard. The whole family can use this kitchen without getting in each other's way.*

2 *Concertina doors open this kitchen and casual living area to a leafy courtyard, creating a very practical zone for entertaining. Having a long breakfast bar and stools is a great alternative to a casual dining table, and in this compact home it also saves space.*

3 *This small, L-shaped arrangement makes the most of the available space. Sleek white cabinetry keeps things visually uncluttered and a fall of sunshine through the skylight is reflected off high-gloss overhead cupboards.*

previous page
Dressing up a meal with fabric napkins and beautiful place settings turns it into a special occasion, no matter how simple the fare.

where you really enjoy being

KITCHENS

TIME WITH FAMILY AND FRIENDS

Rated number one on many a to-do list is spending more time with family and friends; the people that support you, share your deepest feelings and accept you, no matter what. Family units are increasingly diverse, but their importance in people's lives is consistent. Making time to commune on a regular basis will help strengthen the bond and bring balance to your life and theirs.

Yet work and a hectic schedule often take first place. Work is unavoidable for most of us and many parents are overworking to provide a 'better' lifestyle for their children. But can a new toy or overseas holiday compensate for that time apart? Without consistent interaction, the quality time you do make can end up falling short of expectations. You lose touch with each other's interests and end up 'forcing' family fun.

Having time together as a regular part of your day lets bonds form naturally. While it is sometimes easier said than done, sitting down for dinner together provides a time to debrief and share the events of the day. Preparing the food can also become a team effort, taking the pressure off the cook while also stimulating conversation. It may be unachievable every night, but try to make a meal-date once a week that is set in stone.

Defining your dining and social zones encourages interaction. If you don't have a dining room, try using low storage items such as a buffet to delineate the meals area. And don't leave the cook out of the picture – open-plan kitchen/living spaces entice people to the kitchen area, especially if there is a breakfast bar and comfy stools. In the living area, avoid making the television the focal point. Position some chairs away from the television in an arrangement that encourages talk time.

Aside from just talking to each other, try finding activities the whole family can enjoy, such as sport, gardening or DIY projects. Remember, it's not just 'kid time', it's family time – you should enjoy it as well. The need to connect with friends is just as vital. As French poet Eustache Deschamps wrote, 'Friends are relatives you make for yourself.'

Don't be afraid to make the first move and get in touch. Send off a text message or a short email whenever a friend crosses your mind, rather than waiting for that elusive 'free time'. Catching up doesn't have to be a big deal – just getting together for coffee reinforces friendships. Sharing hobbies or sports also makes friend-time a way of life.

You'll find the most important and fun times happen around the kitchen table

1 Deciding on open or closed storage will depend on how much attention you wish your cooking spot to receive. When the kitchen merges with entertaining areas, having closed storage masks the functional nature of the room. However, when the kitchen is to be a focal point, as in this room, displays on open shelves make a creative statement about its purpose.

2 This kitchen is the hub of a contemporary home, melding seamlessly with the living and entertaining areas. Inclusive designs like this are the core of open-plan living. The use of neutral colours emphasises the feeling of space and creates a fluid movement between the different zones.

3 It's not quite an outdoor kitchen, but this room connects with the elements in many ways. A glazed sliding door opens the room to a sheltered verandah and facilitates cross-ventilation, and clerestory windows let sunlight penetrate the space from both sides. The sky-blue cabinetry keeps the interior bright, whatever the weather.

4 Contemporary designs require little decoration, so use utensils as hanging artworks. The stainless-steel splashback here is a great industrial-style backdrop for a collection of kitchen tools. As well as freeing up drawer space, having utensils on a rack also keeps them within easy reach.

1 *Stretching along just one wall of a cottage, this kitchen looks beautiful in bold black. When dealing with dark colours such as this, leave a space between the cabinets and the ceiling to avoid a claustrophobic effect. The large mirror reflects light to brighten the space.*

2 *The first step in designing a kitchen is to examine your lifestyle needs: do you cook often or eat on the go? This area was created for a serious cook, with an extravagance of preparation areas and an easy-to-clean, high-gloss finish. Deep drawers and pull-out shelves provide masses of storage.*

3 *Sinuous lines and dark wenge cabinetry conceal the utilitarian purpose of this space. The rich chocolate and espresso tones are carried through to the living and dining area, and the island bench looks like a piece of freestanding furniture.*

WARM AND COOL YOUR HOME

Feeling comfortable in your home often depends on having the right temperature balance. An ambient temperature of between 18°C and 25°C is considered the most comfortable, with a relative humidity of between 30 and 65 per cent.

A home designed along passive solar design principles traps the sun's light and heat inside in winter, and its interior is shielded from the rays in summer, when the sun is higher in the sky. This natural approach will help cut your power bills, reducing the amount of greenhouse gas your household is responsible for producing – and that's an action sure to make you feel happier.

An important aspect of keeping cool or cosy is good insulation and appropriate window treatments. Insulation keeps heat from escaping through the walls, floors and roof and means you will be saving on fuel bills in winter. Heat loss through windows may be reduced by hanging lined curtains that extend at least 10cm beyond the edge of the window, 15cm above its top, and finish just a couple of centimetres off the floor. In cold climates, glass should be double-glazed, as this halves heat loss. Insulation works in summer by keeping heat out and interiors cool.

For homes that don't benefit from solar orientation, consider energy-efficient reverse-cycle airconditioners – your enjoyment and the long-term environmental savings are well worth the investment. In any case, developing a temperature control system will make staying inside a favoured option.

1 *Having a television or music system in the kitchen makes cooking on your own seem less solitary. This kitchen opens onto the living area, with the island bench positioned so the cook enjoys prime viewing. If the television is actually in the kitchen, place it in an elevated corner position.*

2 *The streamlined design and finishes inspire a clean, unhurried feel in this room. A bi-fold door at one end opens to a plunge pool, and the presence of water reinforces the day-spa vibe of this space. Lustrous surfaces of glass, stainless steel and polished concrete seem to capture the fluidity of the water outside.*

3 *A bold splashback will transform a kitchen from so-so to striking. A cherry-red splashback is an energetic focal point for this room. When using a strong colour or a patterned splashback, team it with sleek surfaces and more muted tones so it retains its impact.*

Please the cooks by giving them a room with a view and a cup of sunshine

3

It's the choice of building materials in a kitchen that defines its style

2

1 A trio of pendant lights illuminates a workbench-cum-breakfast bar and emphasises the cut-off between the casual dining space and the serious cooking zone. Downlights are great companions to pendant lighting as they produce an even general light or may be focused to provide task lighting over work areas.

2 This country kitchen enjoys a gentle breeze and stunning views from every side. When emphasising a view, use a simple interior scheme with muted or neutral tones. Too much white in a sunny room will produce unwanted glare, so team it with timber to soften the glow.

3 A galley-style kitchen is favoured by many chefs as benchtops, cooktop and sink are in close proximity, making cooking easy. Like all kitchens, it needs good lighting to function properly. Here, an adjacent atrium floods the kitchen with sunshine.

4 Timber flooring is increasingly popular in the kitchen and is a simple way to visually unite living and cooking areas. Timber is considered a better 'breather' than synthetic materials, cooling and warming very effectively. A parquetry floor such as this makes for a more individual look.

Being able to turn a garden setting into a dining oasis makes entertaining a breeze

1 *Why go out when you can entertain under the stars, in your own home? This well-lit patio is perfect for night-time alfresco dining. Chair covers are a great way of dressing up outdoor furniture for formal entertaining. Add a few candles for ambience and an outdoor brazier for warmth.*

2 *A few decorative touches can transform a simple garden setting into an enchanting dining oasis. Glass lanterns make this outdoor space feel like an exotic room. Decorative pots and garden sculptures can also be used to introduce a little flair.*

ALFRESCO

ENTERTAINING OUTDOORS

Ask visitors what they most like about Australia and, apart from the scenery and blue skies, it's the relaxed lifestyle. One of the great benefits of being Australian is not being bogged down by hundreds of years of tradition. And that means when you have friends around, they don't stand on ceremony; rather, the aim is for everyone – including you – to have a good time and feel right at home.

This often works best during the warmer months, when you can make the most of the weather and entertain outdoors in the garden or on a balcony. 'Alfresco' may as well be translated as 'relaxed and casual', because that's the result you're aiming for.

Sit-down food is often far easier to make – and deal with – than fiddly finger food. If time is your main concern, you're better off serving a simple pasta with salad and bread than coming up with half a dozen or more bite-sized treats. Another easy alternative is wraps – fresh tortillas or rice-paper rounds surrounded by plates of fillings, including salad, marinated vegetables, slices of cold meats, cheeses and dips. For starters, opt for something light such as baked ricotta served with a fresh salsa, and for dessert it's hard to go past a big bowl of cherries or other seasonal fruit.

If you don't have time to cook everything, pick up a few ready-made items at your local deli or supermarket and add a few personal touches – a scattering of fresh herbs or homemade salads, for instance – to take the dishes to another level.

Make sure you have plenty of everything, from water to wine. Your guests will, more than likely, bring a bottle or two of wine, but don't depend on it. They might surprise you and bring flowers or chocolates instead. You may have chosen a particular wine to suit the meal, but at more casual dinners it's perfectly acceptable to open guests' bottles. And if you'd rather stick to what you've chosen, that's fine as well. Consider the wine a gift from them to you.

If the idea of inviting friends over to dinner fills you with dread, there's always the option of afternoon tea. It might sound like something your grandmother would have done, but often those old-fashioned ideas are best. There's no need to do any of the cooking yourself if you don't want to – buy some delicious cakes, whip up a couple of plates of sandwiches and brew up some tea or coffee. Remember, more than anything, the whole point of getting together over a meal is to stay in touch.

1 The manicured topiary and bright garden beds in this courtyard create a tranquil area in which to unwind or enjoy a drink with friends. In summer, a large Chinese elm provides welcome shade.

2 An internal courtyard is a wonderfully private space in which to entertain. Here, festive lanterns and colourful cushions set the scene for a summer party. The courtyard is also a light well for the home, filling the living area with sunshine.

Serve pre-dinner drinks at the kitchen bar, mains in the courtyard, then retire to

1 *Shapes as well as colours may be contrasted in the garden. Here, beautifully glazed pottery 'boulders' soften the look of a strictly straight-edged pond.*

2 *A creeping fig covering the wall helps turn a courtyard into a cool, green garden room. A pond takes centre stage and is the source of a stream that meanders through the garden. The mudstone slabs used as pavers have a beautiful earthy tone. Although this area is totally manmade, it avoids the harsh edges and glare that can plague an ill-designed courtyard garden.*

SCENTUAL THERAPY

You must have noticed the way a particular scent will transport you straight back to a very specific time and place, in a way nothing else can. Whether it's to a holiday house where you stayed at age 10, or to an office that you worked in when you were 20 is beside the point – smells have an uncanny way of taking you right there. Memories associated with a fragrance – whether good or bad – are more emotionally intense than those triggered by any other type of sensory cue.

Smell is the first sense that you develop, well before sight or hearing become vital parts of your survival mechanism. Humans distinguish around 10,000 different odours, so why not surround yourself with the most pleasant scents you can?

Scientists have discovered that the quickest way to change a person's mood is with a smell. A sniff of lavender or vanilla will make you feel relaxed, even lowering your blood pressure and heart rate. Mixed floral scents apparently increase the speed at which people learn, while the scent of green apples may reduce migraine headaches.

A whole discipline – aromatherapy – has been built up around using the essential oils of plants and flowers to improve physical and emotional wellbeing. The oils work almost entirely through the sense of smell (although tiny quantities also go through the skin and into the bloodstream where they work their magic) and may be used in various ways. A few possibilities to try at home include massage, baths or footbaths (four or five drops of oil added to the water) and in oil-burners.

Energising essential oils include mandarin, bergamot, ginger and tea-tree, while the most calming include sandalwood, vetiver, frankincense and patchouli. It's important that you actually like the scent – you're not going to get any benefit if you find the smell unpleasant, so make sure you take a sniff before buying any particular oil.

While using essential oils is one way of creating lovely scents around the house – and of disguising some less-than-lovely ones – there are plenty of other ways to fill your sanctuary with an appealing aroma. The delicious smell of something cooking – a cake or roast dinner in the oven, or a hearty soup on the stove – is homely and nostalgic, and could immediately take you back to less stressful times. And spending a few dollars on a bunch of hyacinths, sweet peas or other fragrant flowers you love is a small price to pay to have their perfume wafting through your home. Freshly laundered sheets dried in the sun, the scent of timber polish or of a wood fire – it's the simplest things that can revitalise your spirit.

Plan a secret garden with places to sit, eat and meditate; water features bring a

1 This wisteria walk really shows off in early spring. Its dangle of purple blooms adds a flash of brilliance to a mostly green scene. The dark red foliage of a Japanese maple (Acer palmatum var. dissectum) and a snowy Viburnum plicatum also break up the green. Plan your garden as a painter does a picture, using plants to bring different colours to the composition.

2 An unusual stacked-slate fountain is made even more impressive by its setting. The cyclamen-coloured wall at its rear attracts attention to the water feature and contrasts with its dark stone. The surrounds are planted with succulents and low-maintenance grasses.

unique tranquillity

ORGANIC GARDENING

Organic gardening aims to keep the garden free of artificial pesticides and fertilisers, the waterways clean, the soil and food unpolluted, and the garden creatures and humans healthy. It's gardening that works with rather than against the cycles of nature.

You can bring your garden more in tune with the environment by first adding nutrient-rich compost to your soil. This is a great way to recycle food scraps, shredded paper and garden clippings. There are so-called organic pesticides, but the best method of keeping pests at bay is to restore the balance between creatures and plants. Spiders, ladybirds and lizards are all wonderful pest-controllers. And even the most resilient weeds can be tackled with organic mulches, hoeing and hand-weeding.

With organic gardening you won't only taste the difference in your vegetables, you will also be involved in doing something positive for the future of the planet.

1 *A deep blue pot on a stainless-steel plinth is a place to focus the eye and meditate in this water garden. It sits beneath a fall of weeping katsura (Cercidiphyllum japonicum) and beside a planting of Japanese iris; a Japanese maple is behind.*

2 *An aubergine-coloured wall makes a cool contrast to the magnolia tree and Japanese maple in this lazy haven. A star jasmine is just beginning to creep along the trellis, and will eventually pepper the wall with its white flowers. Twin water features bring a soothing sound to this backyard getaway.*

3 *Entertaining is the main purpose of this garden area, with the trees and bamboo used like accessories in a living area. The streamlined table and bench seat are set against the side wall to maximise the amount of standing room for guests.*

mass plantings and plenty of paving

1 *Allow children to create their own sanctuary within the garden. It might be a little treehouse or a tyre hanging from a tree, but it will be a treasured retreat. Scheduling 'outside' time with the children will also stimulate their imagination beyond the television and computer games.*

2 *The owners of this home have encouraged their children's love of horses by creating a place where both kids and ponies are welcome. The stable entrance has a concrete floor for easy cleaning and a rack for riding gear – there's even a chandelier for fun.*

3 *Everyone needs a special place of their own. In this household, a Balinese garden seat is reserved just for the kids. A swinging chair or hammock could also be set up as a quiet place to dream or as a fun spot for sharing stories and playing games.*

BEADED WIND CHIME

YOU'LL NEED

- 4 metres string
- glass beads
- 45cm x 0.6mm-diameter white pole
- drill
- clamp
- trivet
- 60cm ribbon

METHOD

1 Cut seven 50cm lengths of string, then double them over for added strength. You may cut a couple of the lengths shorter or longer, if you prefer to vary the drops on your wind chime.

2 Place the beads in a shallow bowl and begin your selection of beads. Tie a knot at least 5cm from one end of the doubled string (this excess will be used to attach the drop of beads to the trivet later).

3 String the beads, tying a knot to finish off each strand. Trim the string 5mm from the knot.

4 Cut the white pole into three 15cm lengths. Firmly clamping each length, drill through a small hole, 1cm from the top.

5 Thread the string through the poles and attach them to the trivet, allowing a 5mm hanging gap between the trivet and the pole.

6 Attach the bead drops in the same fashion, spreading them around the trivet evenly. Spacing the bead drops and the poles 1/10th of the way around the trivet each time will give a good effect.

7 Cut three 20cm lengths of ribbon, then fold each in half. Pulling the looped end towards you, slide the ribbon over the outside edge of the trivet, then pull the loose ends through the loop and pull the ribbon tight. Repeat with remaining ribbon lengths, positioning them equidistant around the trivet. Knot together the loose ends to make a handle to hang your wind chime.

MAKE IT @ HOME

Bring music to your ears and sparkle to a room with this simple wind chime

MIXED BERRY FLAN

YOU'LL NEED

- 2 sheets frozen sweet shortcrust pastry, defrosted
- 1 egg white, lightly beaten
- 300ml whipping cream
- 2 large egg yolks
- 2 tablespoons caster sugar
- 500g frozen mixed berries, defrosted on paper towels (keep some in reserve, for serving)

METHOD

1 Preheat oven to 200°C (180°C fan-forced oven). Lay one pastry sheet over the centre of a greased 25cm tart tin with a removable bottom. Cut the other sheet into wide strips and finish lining the tin, leaving a 2cm overhang. Press patched pieces together well and fold the overhang back into the tin to make sturdy sides. Prick base all over with a fork. Refrigerate for 30 minutes.

2 Line the pastry base with baking paper and fill with rice or dried beans. Bake for 10 minutes, then take out of the oven and remove the baking paper, rice or beans. Brush the base with egg white, then return it to the oven for 5 minutes to dry out.

3 Combine the cream, egg yolks and sugar in a bowl and whisk until smooth. Spread berries over the pastry base and top with the cream mixture. Place in the oven and immediately reduce the temperature to 190°C (170°C fan-forced oven). Bake until the cream mixture is firm, but still a little wobbly in the middle, about 25 minutes. Serve warm, with extra berries if desired.

MAKE IT @ HOME

A treat always tastes better when it's shared among family and friends

SHARING & CARING

The familiar surroundings of your home impart
a sense of security, but occasionally you need to swap
what you know for something different, and strike
out for broader horizons. It's outside your house that
you find new influences and new inspirations.
~ You need to experience new landscapes and different
cultures. You should taste exotic food, experience
other people's lifestyles and have adventures that teach
you about the world and your place in it. ~ Then you
can bring home the best souvenirs – memories of
flavours, colours and textures, of songs, smiles and
journeys that will keep inspiring you.

EARTH

1 This spectacular coastline, where rugged bushland meets the sea, is part of the unforgettable scenery around Tasmania's Bay of Fires. You can explore the area on a four-day guided walk, finishing at this secluded but comfortable lodge. The surrounding Mt William National Park is home to abundant birdlife, kangaroos, wombats and other fauna – just the place to reconnect with nature.

2 After a night spent virtually under the stars, the Bay of Fires itself beckons. It was given this name by European settlers who saw the campfires of Aboriginals flickering along its shores at night. The area is yours to explore at leisure, however guided kayak tours on Ansons River trace ancient fishing paths and give an insight into the Aboriginals' connection with this beautiful land.

3 The only building in the Mt William National Park is the Bay of Fires Lodge, perched 40 metres above the ocean. The building's sustainable design is in harmony with its surrounds and staying here puts you in touch with the bush without losing out on creature comforts. At night, local food and Tasmanian wine brings a sweet note of civilisation to this pristine experience.

previous page
Wilson Island in Queensland's tropical waters is accessible only by boat and is as close as you can get to the fantasy of being stranded on a desert island – with all the comforts and none of the hardships that implies! Relaxing in a beachside hut, you can watch whales cruise past and turtles coming ashore to lay eggs.

Physically connecting with the land benefits mind, body and soul

WALK THE EARTH

A beautiful landscape has universal appeal. Hung on the wall, pictures of majestic mountains and lush valleys can bring a feeling of serenity in the midst of a busy day. But experiencing the real thing and actually visiting a place revives your spirit in a way nothing else can. The key is to take your time.

Slow to walking pace and you can really savour the sights, sounds, textures and tastes of a travel destination. Whether your steps lead you off beaten paths into outback Australia or across the threshold of a European kitchen, going slowly helps you connect with a country and its people. Given the chance to chat with an Italian farmer over a stone wall, who cares if your shoes get muddy?

Seeing a country by foot also delivers other benefits – keeping both mind and body fit. But how energetic are you? How much are you willing to carry? Do you prefer the company of old friends or the chance to make new ones? Does history interest you more than geology? Quizzing yourself helps identify the right walking holiday for you.

Inn-to-inn walking is growing in popularity because you carry only a daypack and luggage is transferred between each comfortable guesthouse, B&B and inn. (And all that walking is a great excuse for overindulging in local food.) Terrain and climate dictate walk grades and most companies offer guided and self-guided options.

The next step up in walking holidays is hiking between private lodges in national parks, but the heavyweights of accommodated walking are long-distance alpine hikes, such as the Overland Track in Tasmania or the Himalayas. Camping-walking holidays usually involve carrying considerably more than a daypack.

Trekking Mt Everest is considered the pinnacle of physical and mental challenges, but walking the Kokoda Track in Papua New Guinea will also test the strongest wills. Using a porter on such expeditions reduces your load as well as helping the local economy. Hiring a Sherpa in Nepal or a carrier in New Guinea is also a great way to learn about different lives through a new friend.

The gains from active holidays often outlast the trips themselves. They can inspire you to remain active and to make walking or climbing part of your everyday life. You might set up a home gym or join a bushwalking club. And with the new social networks you develop, you might well find companions for another walking holiday.

Collect seashells, pebbles or postcards to keep the memories alive

1 The decommissioned lighthouse at Eddystone Point overlooks the Bay of Fires and now provides both a focal point and a sense of history for walkers in Mt William National Park.

2 Read up on an area before you visit so you better appreciate what makes it unique. Mt William National Park is home to the largest population of grey kangaroos in Tasmania, so keep your eyes open and tread carefully. By taking your time you can uncover the hidden treasures of Mother Nature.

3 Taking time out allows you to tune into the big things in life rather than worrying about daily minutiae. It allows the things that you think are important to rise to the top of your daily list, rather than being lost at the bottom of a crowded schedule. A couple of mornings spent in an idyllic location like this could see you return home filled with new energy and determination to get where you really want to be in life.

4 Shared experiences are a wonderful bond for family and friends. It's not only the scenery that makes a holiday a once in a lifetime experience, but also the people you enjoy it with. Consider keeping a journal of your holiday to complement the usual snapshots; it really will make the memories last. This white granite beach is visited as part of the Bay of Fires four-day walk.

WATER

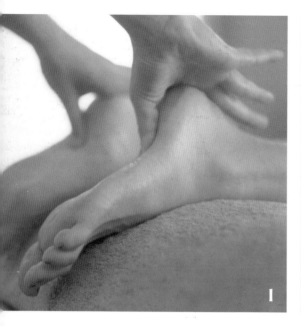

1&2 Up-market resorts offer wonderful day-spa experiences. Book yourself in for a massage – one that goes from head to toe – and feel an amazing release as stress is worked out of your body.

3 Escape to an island paradise and let your tension slip away to the sound of lapping water. Just 20 minutes from Queensland's Gold Coast on South Stradbroke Island is Couran Cove Island Resort. Here you can sleep, play and relax by the water's edge.

4 Explore new activities on your holiday, such as tai chi on the beach. It's just the sort of thing you could continue at home to increase your sense of wellbeing.

Water calms the spirit, whether you're swimming or simply watching the waves

4

REFRESH BODY AND SOUL

A holiday offers an opportunity to restore your sense of equilibrium, and a spa getaway can be the perfect balancer. Surrounded by water, massaged and immersed in it, travellers are encouraged to completely unwind. Yet connecting with water is just the start – modern-day spas use many methods to relax and revive your mind, body and soul, from pampering facials to hot-stone massages, meditation and shiatsu.

Do some research into the style of treatment offered at a spa before you book in, so you don't end up in a shamanistic healing centre when you were after an indulgent facial and seaweed wrap. Five-star resorts in Australia often focus on pampering and relaxation. Aside from facials and therapeutic massages to soothe away stress, you can expect to find a menu of skin treatments, such as mud and mineral wraps, that cleanse the skin and stimulate the lymphatic system.

In Europe, hydrotherapy is hugely popular, with wellness centres dotted throughout the forests of Germany and Austria. Saunas, turkish baths or aromatherapy steam sessions may all be used to relax your body and ease stress.

Massage is another powerful way of promoting a sense of wellbeing. Therapies such as Ayurvedic massage, shiatsu and reflexology form the basis for many new health spas across the globe. However, there's no better place to experience such treatments than in Asia, with Bali and Thailand at the top of the list.

You can re-create a little of that holiday-spa serenity in your own home, too. Add some essential oils to a bath, treat yourself to a daily yoga session or a weekly facial, or create your own Balinese-inspired outdoor room where you can meditate. There are so many ways you can bring a little of a spa's serenity into your own life.

1&2 The spas of Asia are dedicated to the art of relaxation. Water is ever-present in these tropical getaways – from serene lagoons to idyllic beaches, it speaks a language of pure tranquillity. One such retreat is the Anantara Resort Hua Hin, on the Gulf of Siam.

3 Traditional Thai massage is on the menu at Hua Hin. This double massage room, with outdoor terrazzo tub, has a style that could be easily copied for your own sanctuary.

3

ECOTOURISM

As concerns about life on Earth grow, water conservation, recycling and reducing waste are becoming part of day-to-day living. The growth in ecotourism shows that we also want to minimise our impact on the planet during leisure time.

A philosophy of taking only photographs and leaving only footprints helps the forests, deserts, mountains and coasts you explore and the wildlife that inhabits them. It also gives you an understanding of what the planet needs, the importance of balance in nature, and how to tread more lightly. (Wading through a bog is much better for fragile alpine country than extending the damage by walking around it, and more fun.)

Ecotourism choices range from spending a weekend in an energy-efficient hotel that serves meals prepared from an organic garden, to volunteering for a research expedition. Sign on with Earth Watch to excavate the largest burial mound in Poland or collect data to save Australia's endangered Leadbeaters possum, and the cost of your trip supports a host of exploration and research projects around the world. In Australia, look for accommodation, attractions and tours with the eco 'tick' awarded by the National Ecotourism Accreditation Program.

What you bring home from an ecotourism experience can be as different as the trip itself. Close encounters with seals on the Eyre Peninsula in South Australia or removing mites from a stumpy-tailed lizard could inspire study of the animal world. An afternoon with a naturalist on an inland lake may foster plans to replant your suburban backyard with flowering native shrubs to attract birds. Everyone benefits.

NATURE

1 A noisy miner feeds on jacaranda blossom in Sydney. Wild creatures are not restricted to remote areas. Open your eyes and you'll be surprised at who you see.

2 The gorgeous blossoms of a Christmas bush provide a December feast for a galah.

3 A female red-necked wallaby sits in the tall grass at Whiporee, northern New South Wales. Australians are particularly fortunate to be able to see wildlife so close to home. Being aware of their presence is to be aware of the environment, and encourages you to treat both with respect.

4 Spending a few days close to nature can put the world in perspective. In the Yarra Ranges National Park in Victoria, Cement Creek flows over moss-covered boulders and past tree ferns. The beauty held in a small flower or aged eucalypt encourages you to slow down, tread lightly and appreciate the little things in life. In the rainforest, you can stop and be still and listen to nature.

Spending time in an unspoilt place can provide valuable lessons for your daily life

TASTING THE WORLD

A culinary tour can reveal much more than a few new recipes. It enables you to experience the most social aspect of a culture – sharing a meal together. No matter what the society, much interaction takes place over food. It is in the kitchen that many anecdotes from the day are exchanged, where passions flare and where history is shared. To fully experience the world outside your sanctuary, leave the worn tourist road and taste the difference a food tour can make to your journey.

The first thing to take with you is an open mind: food prepared in its country of origin often differs from the versions of ethnic food served up in the West, so you may be in for a few surprises! The language of food will be your guide, so learn a few phrases before you go, especially if you have special dietary requirements.

Beyond that, the food itself is a way of communing with others. To experience a food tour with Australian Aborigines, for example, is to hear a story of their history. Through sharing berries, seeds, bush flowers, wallaby and water gathered from tree roots, you are able to feel their connection to the land. Likewise, a tour of Tuscany is as much about seeing the olive groves and vineyards as sharing food and wine with the locals.

A good food tour will cross over into culture and history and give you a chance to cook like the locals, so shop around for a good package. It also makes its way home to your own kitchen. Keep the flavours alive by creating a herb garden, collecting authentic spices, or seeking out the local community from that culture for the best food and produce. With the right ingredients, you'll cook up a global adventure.

PEOPLE

4

1 Whether it's an artwork hanging in the Louvre or an ancient rock carving, each says something about the place and people who created it and helps you understand a culture and way of life very different from your own. Here, the Wandjina people have painted figures on the walls of a rock shelter near King Edward River, in the Kimberley region of Western Australia.

2 Food often tells a story of the culture. These wattle-flower fritters made with glory wattle (Acacia spectabilis) are a colonial recipe and tell of the influence of European settlers on Australia's indigenous people. Likewise, your food tour may affect the way you cook in your own kitchen, giving you more than memories to take home.

3 Get involved with people by preparing food together. In the Northern Territory, Aborigines grind seeds of mulga (Acacia aneura) and dogwood (A. coriacea) in the traditional way to make children's porridge. Whether you help gather the seeds, grind them or serve the finished meal, participating is a way to bridge the gap between different languages and cultures.

4 In travelling to the source of a food, you'll taste much more than the local flavours. Here, the beautiful colours of Windjana Gorge in the Kimberley region mesmerise visitors. By listening to the stories of its traditional owners, you can learn so much more about this land.

You share your heart when you share a table with a stranger

WEEKENDS AWAY

Bored with your job? Growing apart from your partner? Losing your focus? Going away is not an extravagance, it is essential therapy. Taking time out from your over-organised home and work life has enormous benefits.

Escaping a too-familiar environment and everyday routine gives you a chance to re-evaluate issues that have been bugging you; to see from a new perspective an annoying colleague or the loss of a favourite jumper in a too-hot wash. Relaxed, rested and well fed, you can reconnect with a side of yourself you may have thought lost, or rediscover your partner as the person you originally fell in love with.

Forget about your renovations, promotion and in-laws. Talk about the dessert menu, the books you just bought, where you would like to go on your second honeymoon – or first! – and which of the bushwalks you might do tomorrow.

Even a short break will help you face work challenges and solve problems more calmly. It can improve your relationship and strengthen family ties, leading to more loving and laughing together. And you don't have to go far – here are just a few ideas.

Enjoy a weekend for two in a country house renowned for cooking. Lie in late and breakfast in bed before visiting a vineyard or three. Escape to the ocean to taste the salt air on your lips and feed each other from a paper parcel of fish and chips.

Take a spa-room package at a luxury city hotel and indulge your passions for food, wine and each other. Cruise the tranquil world of river red gums and eagles on a houseboat. You can also take advantage of cheap airfares and maroon yourself on a Fijian island just to watch the setting sun silhouette the coconut palms. The world is there for you to discover, even if it's just a weekend visit down the road.

1, 2&3 Peppers Retreats and Resorts owns and runs a collection of boutique hotels around Australia. Each has its own flavour. Pepper's Hidden Vale near Brisbane (1&3) is on a Queensland cattle property, while Peppers Casuarina Lodge (2) is in the middle of a rainforest in the Byron Bay area. They are favourite destinations for couples wanting to get away for a weekend or longer.

4 Bedarra Island Resort in the Whitsundays is set among unspoiled bushland. Bedrooms open onto a private deck with a plunge pool. There's nothing to disturb your relaxation except the sound of the sea lapping on the shore and the calling of the native birds. Bliss!

Going away with your partner is good therapy for a relationship

4

CULTURE

1 Rome's Colosseum, dating from 72AD, is the world's largest amphitheatre. You will be inspired by the scale of the building and the colourful history contained within its walls. And while you won't see a lion, the stray cats that live here today are an ironic connection to the past.

2 The Santa Maria della Salute church stands at the entrance to Venice's Grand Canal, in the middle of a city which essentially hasn't changed for centuries. Venice was once the world's trading centre and there are many wares tied closely to its art and history that delight the senses. Watch a Murano glass-blower, try on an ornate Venetian mask and visit Piazza San Marco (St Mark's Square) to feel the history come alive.

Old-world art and architecture are a wonderful way to connect to the European soul

A EUROPEAN TOUR

Literary classics and lavish costume dramas evoke the riches of European culture and breathe life into a romantic world far removed from our own. But like the young ladies in novels who finish their education with a grand tour of Italy, you'll find nothing compares with actually seeing the original masterpieces, sculptures and architecture.

Picasso's genius shines in a Spanish setting. The Parisian sun shows the cathedral of Notre Dame at its best. And you can only fully appreciate Michelangelo's sculpture 'David' when standing at his feet in Florence.

Travel can show you art through the ages. It broadens your mind and gives you cultural references, opening new avenues of conversation when meeting people. It may even entice you to purchase some original works yourself.

You can plan your own grand European tour, seeking out local guides for cultural highlights, or join a group led by an art historian or lecturer. You could see works in progress in art studios, discover the contemporary vision of the Guggenheim Museum in Bilbao in Spain, or delve into the treasury of handcrafts, precious metalwork and decorative arts in the Victoria & Albert Museum in London.

A grand gallery tour might include the Louvre in Paris to see Leonardo da Vinci's famous portrait, 'Mona Lisa', St Petersburg to wander the Hermitage's corridors, and Florence to swoon over Botticelli angels in the Uffizi.

The spirit of these individual masterpieces and the political and artistic movements that inspired them can be traced back to the Mediterranean birthplace of Western civilisation, Greece, so it would be an appropriate place to end a tour.

When you stand among columns in a temple ruin or read Homer's *Iliad* in a 4th-century BC theatre, the classical style is no longer a concept – it has shape and texture. It comes alive as architecture, statuary and pottery, leaving you with a sense of European culture that outlives many other memories of your travels.

1 *Portugal's Mosteiro dos Jerónimos, in a suburb of Lisbon, is one of the finest remaining examples of Portuguese Renaissance-Gothic architecture. The monastery's grandeur is a reminder of Portugal's wealth and importance in the 1500s.*

2 *The Duomo in Milan, Europe's largest Gothic cathedral, took 500 years to complete. It contains an incredible range of artworks by some of Europe's most famous painters. It is often said that art is food for the soul and in Europe you can truly feast.*

3 *The Louvre contains one of the most important art collections in the world and is on most tourists' must-see list for Paris. The former palace contains everything from ancient artefacts to modern masterpieces. A day spent meandering through this incredible collection will give you an insight into the European psyche.*

3

ACKNOWLEDGMENTS

P: Photographer
A: Architecture
ID: Interior design
S: Styling

FRONT COVER
P: Sharyn Cairns A: Russell Casper, Grodski Architects, Prahran, Vic.
Pgs 2-3
P: Sharyn Cairns ID: TD Interiors, Collingwood, Vic.
Pg 5
P: Simon Kenny

CONTENTS
Pgs 6-7
From left: P: Eric Victor-Perdraut; P: Sharyn Cairns; P: Simon Kenny; P: Phil Aynsley; P: Simon Kenny; P: Andrew Lehmann

UNWIND & IMAGINE
Pg 8
P: Eric Victor-Perdraut A: Elizabeth Watson-Brown, St Lucia, Qld. Builder: Ron Sutton Building Company Pty Ltd, Murwillumbah, NSW.
FRONT OF HOUSE
Pgs 10-11
1. P: Dan Magree 2. P: Sharyn Cairns A: Cunningham Top Architects, Malvern, Vic. Builder: M&M Lowe Constructions, Frankstown, Vic.
Pgs 12-13
1. P: Dan Magree Garden design: Margit Wright, Adelaide Garden Design, Inglewood, SA. 2. P: Dan Magree Garden design: Margit Wright, Adelaide Garden Design, Inglewood, SA.
HALLWAYS
Pgs 14-15
1. P: Karin Calvert-Borshoff D: Yael K Designs (building designs) and Yael K Furniture Design & Manufacture, Coolbinia, WA. Artworks: silver vase by Carol Bouys; lacquered steel sculpture by Matthew Carney; 'Millennium 2' vase by Mary Mack.
2. P: Dan Magree D: Patrick Meneguzzi, Toorak, Vic. Artwork: 'Lover's Kiss' by Maggie Sheppard.
Pgs 16-17
1. P: Dan Magree A: Centrum Architects, South Yarra, Vic. Builder: Heber the Builder, South Yarra, Vic. Artwork: Zimbabwean sculpture from Chapungu Shona Gallery.
2. P: David Morcombe A: Icon Group,

Cottesloe, WA. ID: LCD Interiors, Bicton, WA. Artwork: Keren Seelander.
3. P: Neil Lorimer ID: Geoffrey Brown & Associates, Hawthorn, Vic.
LIVING ROOMS
Pgs 18-19
1. P: David Morcombe A: Icon Group, Cottesloe, WA. ID: LCD Interiors, Bicton, WA. 2. P: Dan Magree
Pgs 20-21
1. P: Dan Magree ID: Sheraton House Interior Design, Armadale, Vic. 2. P: Simon Kenny A: Jason Blake Architecture, Camperdown, NSW. Artwork: Ken Walk. 3. P: Dan Magree A: Col Bandy, Albert Park, Vic. Artworks: George Wallaby. 4. P: David Morcombe
Pgs 22-23
1. P: Dan Magree A: Greenway Hirst Page Architects, Melbourne, Vic. ID: TD Interiors, Melbourne, Vic. Landscape designer: Jack Merlo Design, Melbourne, Vic.
2. P: Eric Victor-Perdraut ID: Stephen Kidd Design, Sunshine Beach, Qld.
MEDIA ROOMS
Pgs 24-25
1. P: Andrew Lehmann ID: Basicz, Sydney, NSW. 2. P: Andrew Lehmann A: Eeles Trelease, Newtown, NSW. Builder: Les Harris, Carlingford, NSW.
3. P: Andrew Lehmann ID: Alexandra McKenzie Interiors, Elizabeth Bay, NSW.
DECKS & VERANDAHS
Pgs 26-27
1. P: Simon Kenny 2. P: Sharyn Cairns 3. P: Eric Victor-Perdraut A: Elizabeth Watson-Brown, St Lucia, Qld. Builder: Ron Sutton Building Company Pty Ltd, Murwillumbah, NSW. 4. P: Eric Sierens
Pgs 28-29
1. P: Dan Magree 2. P: Dan Magree 3. P: Simon Kenny 4. P: Dan Magree
MAKE IT @ HOME
Pgs 30-31
P: Andrew Lehmann S: Amanda Talbot Project by Amanda Talbot
Pgs 32-33
P: Andrew Lehmann S: Amanda Talbot Project by Amanda Talbot

REFLECT & RELEASE
Pg 34
P: Sharyn Cairns A: Russell Casper, Grodski Architects, Prahran, Vic.
BATHROOMS
Pgs 36-37
1. P: Andrew Elton ID: Bridget Tyer, Neutral Bay, NSW. 2. P: Andrew Elton

Pgs 38-39
1. P: Simon Kenny A: Gary Lewin, Balmain, NSW. ID: Deborah Muddle, North Sydney, NSW. 2. P: Rodney Weidland 3. P: Andrew Elton D: M-Design Tiles & Bathroom, Fyshwick, ACT. Builder: Paul Howick, Florey, ACT.
Pgs 40-41
1. P: JH Photography D: AVJennings, nationwide.
2. P: Dan Magree A: Centrum Architects, South Yarra, Vic. Builder: Heber the Builder, South Yarra, Vic.
SWIMMING POOLS
Pgs 42-43
1. P: Eric Victor-Perdraut A: Elizabeth Watson Brown, St Lucia, Qld. Builder: Ron Sutton Building Company Pty Ltd, Murwillumbah, NSW. 2. P: David Morcombe A: Colliere Menkens Pickwell Architecture, Northbridge, WA.
Pgs 44-45
1. P: Trevor Fox 2. P: David Morcombe A: Hofman and Brown Architects, Cottesloe, WA. 3. P: Brett Boardman A: Nicholas Murcutt Architects, Sydney, NSW.
Pgs 46-47
1. P: Eric Victor-Perdraut 2. P: Eric Victor-Perdraut A: Elizabeth Watson Brown, St Lucia, Qld. Builder: Ron Sutton Building Company Pty Ltd, Murwillumbah, NSW. 3. P: Leon Bird A: TAG Architects, Perth, WA. 4. P: Phil Aynsley
DAY SPAS
Pgs 48-49
1. P: Andre Martin 2. P: Simon Kenny A: Davis Ye Architects, Zetland, NSW.
Pgs 50-51
1. P: Eric Victor-Perdraut A: Gabriel & Elizabeth Poole Design, Noosaville, Qld. 2. P: Phil Aynsley A: Utz Sanby Architects, Crows Nest, NSW.
3. P: Rodney Weidland
4. P: Andrew Elton
MAKE IT @ HOME
Pgs 54-55
P: Andrew Lehmann S: Amanda Talbot Project by Amanda Talbot
Pgs 56-57
P: Andrew Lehmann S: Amanda Talbot Project by Amanda Talbot

REST & RELAX
Pg 58
P: Simon Kenny
Pgs 60-61
1. P: Dan Magree Artwork: 'Dozing Woman' by Donna Richie.
2. P: Simon Kenny

Pgs 62-63
1. P: Chris Bennett 2. P: Dan Magree 3. P: Dan Magree 4. P: Dan Magree ID: Danielle Trippett Interior Design, Albert Park, Vic.
Pgs 64-65
1. P: John Best D: Urban Pad, Windsor, Vic. Artwork: 'Woodscape' by Fleur Bouw. 2. P: Dean Wilmot 3. P: Dan Magree 4. P: Dan Magree ID: Danielle Trippett Interior Design, Albert Park, Vic.
Pgs 66-67
1. P: Simon Kenny 2. P: Dan Magree ID: Jennie Goble, pomp, St Kilda, Vic. Artworks: 'Cakes' by Gavin Brown.
Pgs 68-69
1. P: Andrew Lehmann ID: Alexandra McKenzie Interiors, Elizabeth Bay, NSW.
2. P: Warwick Kent ID: Alma Maccallum, Sydney, NSW. 3. P: Simon Griffiths Trompe l'oeil: Grand Illusions.
ENSUITES
Pgs 70-71
1. P: Chris Bennett 2. P: Rodney Weidland
WALK-IN ROBES
Pgs 72-73
1. P: Dan Magree
STORAGE
Pgs 74-75
1. P: Dan Magree 2. P: Dan Magree A: Centrum Architects, South Yarra, Vic.
Pgs 76-77
1. P: Trevor Fox A: Salt Studio Architects, Glenelg, SA D: Arbon Design, Hyde Park, SA. 2. P: Andrew Lehmann 3. P: Dan Magree
Pgs 78-79
1. P: Ray Clarke 2. P: Trevor Fox A: Salt Studio Architects, Glenelg, SA D: Arbon Design, Hyde Park, SA. 3. P: Trevor Fox
MAKE IT @ HOME
Pgs 80-81
P: Andrew Lehmann S: Amanda Talbot Project by Jacqui Winn
Pgs 82-83
P: Andrew Lehmann S: Amanda Talbot Project by Jacqui Winn

REVIVE & RELISH
Pg 84
P: Phil Aynsley
PERSONAL SPACES
Pgs 85-86
1. P: Simon Kenny A: Misho & Associates, East Sydney, NSW.
2. P: Dan Magree
Pgs 87-88
1. P: Dan Magree 2. P: Andrew Lehmann

3. **P:** Dan Magree 4. **P:** Dan Magree
Pgs 90-91
1. **P:** Jeff Kilpatrick **ID:** Russell Grainger, St Kilda, Vic. 2. **P:** Dan Magree
3. **P:** Simon Kenny 4. **P:** Dan Magree
Pgs 92-93
1. **P:** David Morcombe 2. **P:** Dan Magree **ID:** Jane Agnew Interior Design, Cottesloe, WA.
SUNROOMS
Pgs 94-95
1. **P:** Patrick Reynolds Photography
2. **P:** Dan Magree
Pgs 96-97
1. **P:** Dan Magree 2. **P:** Bill Anagrius **A:** DHG International, Sydney, NSW.
3. **P:** Russell Brooks **A:** Raymond Teo, Sydney, NSW.
READING ROOMS
Pgs 98-99
1. **P:** Dan Magree 2. **P:** Simon Kenny
3. **P:** Dan Magree 4. **P:** Simon Kenny
HOME WORK
Pgs 100-101
1. **P:** Phil Aynsley 2. **P:** Simon Kenny
Pgs 102-103
1. **P:** Dan Magree **ID:** Blend Design, Collingwood, Vic. 2. **P:** Dan Magree
3. **P:** David Morcombe **ID:** Judith Barrett-Lenard Designs, Dalkeith, WA.
4. **P:** Dan Magree
Pgs 104-105
1. **P:** Dan Magree **A:** Robert Ficarra, Interlandi Mantesso Architects, Richmond, Vic. Artwork: Cristina Torchia.
2. **P:** Dan Magree
3. **P:** Dan Magree **ID:** Danielle Trippett Interior Design, Albert Park, Vic.
GARDEN SHEDS
Pgs 106-107
1. **P:** Dan Magree 2. **P:** Michael McCoy
Pgs 108-109
2. **P:** Simon Griffiths
MAKE IT @ HOME
Pgs 110-111
P: Andrew Lehmann **S:** Amanda Talbot Project by Amanda Talbot
Pgs 112-113
P: Andrew Lehmann **S:** Amanda Talbot Project by Amanda Talbot

ENERGISE &EXCITE
Pg 114
P: Simon Kenny
FAMILY ROOMS
Pgs 116-117
1. **P:** Dan Magree 2. **P:** Andrew Elton **A:** Interform Design Construct, Kingston, ACT. Artwork: Craig Easton.

Pgs 118-119
1. **P:** Simon Kenny 2. **P:** Simon Kenny **A:** Su Keong Design Architects, North Narrabeen, NSW. 3. **P:** Bill Anagrius Artwork: Letterman. 4. **P:** Dan Magree
5. **P:** Phil Aynsley **A:** Larcombe + Solomon Architects, Surry Hills + NSW. **ID:** Carroll and Carroll, Waverley, NSW. Artwork: painting over sofa by Angela Brennan; 'May Morning' by Rosalie Gascoigne.
FORMAL LIVING
Pgs 120-121
1. **P:** Eric Victor-Perdraut **ID:** Stephen Kidd Design, Sunshine Beach, Qld. Artwork: Gordon Richards. 2. **P:** Simon Kenny
3. **P:** Simon Kenny **ID:** Ruth Levine Designs, Paddington, NSW. Artwork: 'Whistler's Morning' by Richard Allen; 'Evoluta II' sculpture by Roger Apte.
4. **P:** Andrew Elton
Pgs 122-123
1. **P:** Rodney Weidland 2. **P:** Andrew Lehmann
TRANSITION ZONES
Pg 124-125
1. **P:** Phil Aynsley 2. **P:** Trevor Fox **A:** Dimitty Andersen, Adelaide, SA.
Pgs 126-127
1. **P:** Trevor Fox 2. **P:** David Morcombe
3. **P:** David Morcombe **A:** Colin Moore, Subiaco, WA. Landscaping: Tim Davies Landscaping, Osborne Park, WA.
DINING ROOMS
Pgs 128-129
1. **P:** Dan Magree **ID:** Rick Davis, Habitat, Melbourne, Vic. 2. **P:** Dan Magree
Pgs 130-131
1. **P:** Trevor Fox **A:** Max Pritchard, Kingston Park, SA.
Pgs 132-133
1. **P:** Andre Martin **A:** Peter Burford, Newtown, NSW. **ID:** Bofinger Design, Camperdown, NSW. 2. **P:** Dan Magree **A:** Anthea Bickford Architect, Prahran, Vic. **ID:** Inhabiting Flair, East Malvern, Vic. Artwork: Graham Fransella.
Pgs 134-135
1. **P:** Maree Homer 2. **P:** Simon Griffiths Architect: Ian James Smith Architects, Camberwell, Vic. **ID:** Aisance Design, Camberwell, Vic.
MAKE IT @ HOME
Pgs 136-137
P: Andrew Lehmann **S:** Amanda Talbot Project by Amanda Talbot
Pgs 138-139
P: Andrew Lehmann **S:** Amanda Talbot Project by Amanda Talbot

ENJOY & ENTERTAIN
Pg 140
P: Andrew Lehmann
KITCHENS
Pgs 142-143
1. **P:** Phil Aynsley **ID:** Imodo Design, Manly, NSW. 2. **P:** Andrew Lehmann **ID:** Emily Loxton Interiors, East Sydney, NSW.
3. **P:** Andrew Lehmann **ID:** Greg Natale, Surry Hills, NSW.
Pgs 144-145
1. **P:** David Morcombe 2. **P:** Phil Aynsley **ID:** Lara Calder, Greenwich, NSW.
3. **P:** Trevor Fox **A:** Max Pritchard, Kingston Park, SA. 4. **P:** Dan Magree **A:** Harwood Architecture, St Kilda, Vic.
Pgs 146-147
1. **P:** Ray Clarke **D:** Jilly Hampshire
2. **P:** Jeff Kilpatrick **ID:** Richard Gasking Interiors, Armadale, Vic. 3. **P:** Dan Magree **ID:** Urban Pad, Windsor Vic.
Pgs 148-149
1. **P:** Dan Magree 2. **P:** Warwick Kent **D:** Buzacott Ocolison Associates, Surry Hills, NSW. 3. **P:** Eric Victor-Perdraut **ID:** Roberta Treffene Interiors, Bardon, Qld.
Pgs 150-151
1. **P:** Trevor Fox 2. **P:** Phil Aynsley **A:** Edward Szewczyk & Associates, Queens Park, NSW. 3. **P:** Dan Magree **A:** Col Bundy, Albert Park, Vic.
4. **P:** Andre Martin **A:** Campbell Luscombe Folk Lichtman, Redfern, NSW.
ALFRESCO
Pgs 152-153
1. **P:** Trevor Fox 2. **P:** Dan Magree
Pgs 154-155
1. **P:** Sharyn Cairns 2. **P:** David Morcombe **A:** Odden Rodrigues Architects, Claremont, WA.
GARDENS
Pgs 156-157
1. **P:** Dan Magree Artwork: clayworks by Ted Secombe, Yarra Glen, Vic.
2. **P:** Peter Clark Garden design: Black Bamboo Landscape Design & Construction, Glen Iris, Vic.
Pgs 158-159
1. **P:** Dan Magree 2. **P:** Dan Magree Fountain built by Harry Brockwell, Ochre Landscape, Guys Hill, Vic.
Pgs 160-161
1. **P:** Dan Magree Artworks: pot by Ted Secombe, Yarra Glen, Vic. 2. **P:** Dan Magree Garden design: Out From the Blue, Hawthorn, Vic. 3. **P:** Dan Magree Garden design: Jack Merlo Landscape Design & Construction, Brighton, Vic.
Pgs 162-163
1. **P:** Dan Magree 2. **P:** Dan Magree

3. **P:** Dan Magree
MAKE IT @ HOME
Pgs 164-165
P: Andrew Lehmann **S:** Amanda Talbot Project by Amanda Talbot
Pgs 166-167
P: Andrew Lehmann **S:** Amanda Talbot Recipe: Loukie Werle

SHARING & CARING
Pg 168
P: David Matheson
EARTH
Pgs 170-171
1. **P:** Simon Kenny 2. **P:** Simon Kenny
3. **P:** Simon Kenny More information at www.bayoffires.com.au
Pgs 172-173
1. **P:** Esther Beaton 2. **P:** Esther Beaton
3. **P:** Esther Beaton 4. **P:** Esther Beaton
WATER
Pgs 174-175
All photos **P:** Courtesy of Couran Cove Island Resort, South Stradbroke Island, Qld. More information at www.courancove.com.au
Pgs 176-177
All photos **P:** Courtesy of Anantara Resort & Spa, Hua Hin, Thailand. More information at www.anantara.com
NATURE
Pgs 178-179
1. **P:** Esther Beaton 2. **P:** Esther Beaton
3. **P:** Esther Beaton 4. **P:** Esther Beaton
PEOPLE
Pgs 180-181
1. **P:** Esther Beaton 2. **P:** Esther Beaton
3. **P:** Esther Beaton 4. **P:** Esther Beaton
Pgs 182-183
1. **P:** Courtesy of Peppers Retreats and Resorts 2. **P:** Courtesy of Peppers Retreats and Resorts
3. **P:** Courtesy of Peppers Retreats and Resorts. More information at www.peppers.com.au
4. **P:** David Matheson
CULTURE
Pgs 184-185
1. **P:** Getty Images 2. **P:** Getty Images
Pgs 186-187
1. **P:** Getty Images 2. **P:** Getty Images
3. **P:** Getty Images

INDEX

AUSTRALIAN HOUSE & GARDEN: SANCTUARY
Editorial director Anny Friis
Editor Alexandra Neuman
Picture research Rosanne Peach
Text Rosanne Peach, Leta Keens, Melanie Ball, Rose-Marie Hillier,
Deborah Hunt, Kylie Imeson, Rowena Mary, Jo McKinnon

ACP BOOKS
Creative director Hieu Chi Nguyen
Copy editor Jo McKinnon
Sales director Brian Cearnes
Publishing manager (rights & new projects) Jane Hazell
Marketing director Nicole Pizanis
Marketing manager Katie Graham
Brand manager Renée Crea
Sales & marketing coordinator Gabrielle Botto
Production manager Carol Currie
Business manager Seymour Cohen
Business analyst Martin Howes
Studio manager Caryl Wiggins
Pre-press Harry Palmer
Editorial coordinator Merryn Pearse
Group publisher Pat Ingram
Publisher Sue Wannan
Editorial director Susan Tomnay
Chief executive officer John Alexander

Produced by **ACP**books
Printed by SNP Leefung, China
Published by ACP Publishing Pty Limited,
54 Park St, Sydney; GPO Box 4088,
Sydney, NSW 2001.
Ph: (02) 9282 8618 Fax: (02) 9267 9438.
acpbooks@acp.com.au
www.acpbooks.com.au
AUSTRALIA: Distributed by Network Services, GPO Box 4088, Sydney, NSW 2001.
Ph: (02) 9282 8777 Fax: (02) 9264 3278.
UNITED KINGDOM: Distributed by Australian Consolidated Press (UK), Moulton Park Business
Centre, Red House Road,
Moulton Park, Northampton, NN3 6AQ.
Ph: (01604) 497531 Fax: (01604) 497533 acpukltd@aol.com
CANADA: Distributed by Whitecap Books Ltd,
351 Lynn Avenue, North Vancouver, BC, V7J 2C4.
Ph: (604) 980 9852 Fax: (604) 980 8197
customerservice@whitecap.ca
www.whitecap.ca
NEW ZEALAND: Distributed by Netlink Distribution Company, ACP Media Centre,
Cnr Fanshawe and Beaumont streets, Westhaven, Auckland.
PO Box 47906, Ponsonby, Auckland, NZ.
Ph: (09) 366 9966 ask@ndcnz.co.nz

Australian House & Garden: Sanctuary.
Includes index.
ISBN 1 86396 412 6.
1. Interior decoration. 2. Gardens.
747.0994
© ACP Publishing Pty Ltd 2005
ABN 18 053 273 546
This publication is copyright. No part of it may be reproduced or transmitted in any form without the
written permission of the publishers.

Front cover: Photography by Sharyn Cairns